W9-BCO-803

3 1218 00415 7047

DATE DUE

ISAMU NOGUCHI

ASIAN AMERICANS OF ACHIEVEMENT

Margaret Cho

Daniel Inouye

Michelle Kwan

Bruce Lee

Maya Lin

Yo-Yo Ma

Isamu Noguchi

Amy Tan

Vera Wang

Kristi Yamaguchi

ASIAN AMERICANS
OF ACHIEVEMENT

ISAMU NOGUCHI

CAROLINE TIGER

CHELSEA HOUSE
PUBLISHERS
An imprint of Infobase Publishing

Isamu Noguchi

Copyright © 2007 by Infobase Publishing

Chelsea House
An imprint of Infobase Publishing
132 West 31st Street
New York, NY 10001

ISBN-10: 0-7910-9276-3
ISBN-13: 978-0-7910-9276-7

Library of Congress Cataloging-in-Publication Data
Tiger, Caroline.
   Isamu Noguchi / Caroline Tiger.
       p. cm.—(Asian Americans of achievement)
   Includes bibliographical references.
   ISBN 0-7910-9276-3 (hardcover)
   1. Noguchi, Isamu, 1904–1988—Juvenile literature. 2. Japanese American sculptors—Biography—Juvenile literature. I. Noguchi, Isamu, 1904–1988.
II. Title. III. Series.
NB237.N6T54 2007
709.2—dc22
[B]
2006026230

Chelsea House books are available at special discounts when purchased in bulk quantities for businesses, associations, institutions, or sales promotions. Please call our Special Sales Department in New York at (212) 967-8800 or (800) 322-8755.

You can find Chelsea House on the World Wide Web at http://www.chelseahouse.com

Text design by Erika K. Arroyo
Cover design by Ben Peterson

Printed in the United States of America
Bang NMSG 10 9 8 7 6 5 4 3 2 1

This book is printed on acid-free paper.

All links and Web addresses were checked and verified to be correct at the time of publication. Because of the dynamic nature of the Web, some addresses and links may have changed since publication and may no longer be valid.

CONTENTS

Boy From Nowhere

"I am going to take Baby for a little trip across the Pacific Ocean about Feb. 1st," Leonie Gilmour wrote in a letter to a friend in January 1907. The baby in Leonie's letter would grow up to be world-famous artist Isamu (pronounced "Samoo") Noguchi, but in early 1907, when he was a little more than two years old, Isamu still didn't have a name. His mother referred to him as "Baby" or as "Yo," which was both a shortened version of his father's name, Yonejiro, and of "Yosemite," a place Yonejiro had been to and written poetry about.

Until his ocean voyage, little Yo lived in a small house at the foot of the San Gabriel Mountains in Pasadena, California, with his mother, Leonie Gilmour, and with her sister and mother. They were far away from his father, Yonejiro Noguchi, a Japanese poet who had returned to his homeland before Isamu was born. They were also far from New York, the place where his American mother and Japanese father had met and lived when they were first married.

They were moving to Japan because Leonie was growing worried about the rising resentment in California toward the Japanese immigrants who were flooding the state. The bad feelings were fanning the flames of discrimination toward the immigrants and their families. In 1905, the California legislature passed a law forbidding intermarriage between whites and "Mongolians," or people of Asian descent. In a nearby town a Japanese boy was arrested for writing a love note to a white schoolmate. In 1906, the San Francisco school board barred Japanese children from attending regular schools. This hostile environment made Leonie afraid of the consequences of raising Yo, a half-American, half-Japanese boy, in California.

In his letters to Leonie, Yonejiro had asked her to bring their baby to Japan so that he could grow up with a father. She was hesitant—she had no family or friends there, and they were happy in America. The rising tide of discrimination, however, prompted her to reconsider. Yonejiro also continued to promise to send a name for their son, but for some reason, he kept putting it off. So when Leonie and Isamu boarded the S.S. *Mongolia* in San Francisco en route to Japan on March 9, 1907, he was still just "Yo."

The ship carried 350 first-class passengers, 68 second-class passengers, and 1,400 third-class passengers. Those in third-class, such as Leonie and Yo, traveled on the lower deck, packed like sardines into tiny cabins, each with two sets of double bunk beds. Leonie and Yo's chamber was in a very uncomfortable spot, right beneath the clanging, overheated boiler room. During most of the 17-day voyage, Yo felt too seasick to eat.

When the ship reached Yokohama, a port city south of Tokyo, Yonejiro hurried onboard to meet his half-American son for the first time. Little Yo was too tired from the journey to give his papa a proper greeting. When the child wouldn't look up at him, Yonejiro was disappointed. He finally did give his boy a name, though. He decided to call him Isamu, which means "brave" or "courageous" in Japanese.

This photograph shows a section of Yokohama, a port city south of Tokyo, at the turn of the twentieth century. Isamu Noguchi and his mother sailed there from the United States to live with Isamu's father.

Until the spring of 1907, Isamu had only known America, but it didn't take him long to become accustomed to life in Tokyo. He loved the sliding *shoji* screens in his new home, and he'd amuse himself by sliding them open and closed while making shadows on the paper as the sun set at the end of the day. Isamu continued to speak English with Leonie, and he also learned Japanese. His first Japanese word was *banzai*, a cheer that means "hurrah" or "long life!"

Still, Isamu didn't forget America. Even at such a young age, Isamu understood that he was a product of both lands. When his mother would ask him, "Are you an American baby?" he'd answer "Yes." And when she'd ask him "Are you a Japanese baby?" he'd reply, again, "Yes."

Isamu seemed to accept the duality of his heritage without question early in his life, but later, the matter became much more complex. The questions "Am I American? Am I Japanese?" took on deeper meaning. What did it mean to be an American? What did it mean to be Japanese? These issues became especially difficult during the times in Isamu's life when America and Japan were at odds and even at war. Complicating Isamu's feelings for his mother's and father's native lands was the way the Japanese and American people received him. It pained Isamu that, although he lived in both countries for extended periods of time at different points in his life, he never felt completely accepted in either place.

At age 69, during an interview quoted in Masayo Duus's *The Life of Isamu Noguchi, Journey Without Borders*, he remarked, "[F]or one with a background like myself the question of identity is very uncertain. And I think it was only in art that it was ever possible for me to find my identity at all." During a life filled with unease about where he really belonged, Isamu found comfort in his art. Through his garden designs, theater sets, paintings, and sculptures, he expressed his feelings about his nationality, his friends, his girlfriends, his family, nature, politics, war, discrimination—basically, about everything under the sun, or at least everything with which he came in contact. Through his art he was able to feel as though he was part of a community, the global community of artists. Artists, he said, "are all pariahs [or outcasts] to start with. And I, being a pariah, was among pariahs and was no longer a pariah."

Isamu discovered art about the time he and his mother found out that Yonejiro had been lying to them. It turned out that Yonejiro had been leading a double life. All along, he had a Japanese family—another wife and baby, and he ultimately chose to live with that family instead of with Leonie and Isamu. Isamu was five years old when Yonejiro had his first son with his Japanese wife. Yonejiro inserted the name of his Japanese son in the household register as "eldest son" instead

Isamu's father, Yonejiro Noguchi, in 1913, several years after he had abandoned his American wife and first son.

of Isamu's, however—a clear sign that he considered the other family more "official."

Leonie had been working as a private English tutor since she'd arrived. When she got a job as an English teacher at a girls' school, she and Isamu moved out of his father's house in northern Tokyo and into a cottage surrounded by greenery and fields, on the south side of the city. When they moved, his mother enrolled him in a new kindergarten nearby. The school was housed in a mansion that a wealthy businessman, Ichizaemon Morimura, had turned into a kindergarten and elementary school. The school was modern for its time—it emphasized the importance of each student's individuality. It was much different from the kindergarten Isamu had previously attended, where he'd felt the need to shave his head so that his curly black hair wouldn't stand out among all the straight-haired boys.

In the early 1900s, few foreigners lived in Japan. Isamu and his mother were oddities. People from miles around would gossip about the American woman and her baby, and everyone knew which house belonged to "Mama-san" and "Baby-san." Leonie, especially, was a spectacle—a white woman in full skirts stood out among Japanese women wearing kimonos and traditional dress. This white woman was living on her own, which, in their eyes, made her even odder. In addition, though he was half-Japanese, Isamu still looked much different from other children. There was that curly hair, and his eyes were round. The other children's eyes were almond shaped.

In a photo from 1911 from his Morimura Kindergarten graduation, Isamu's unique features make him easy to spot. So does his rakish pose. The other little boys and girls hold their diplomas uniformly at their waists, but Isamu holds his up to his mouth and seems to be blowing through it, as if it were a flute. You can tell that he is feeling free and is comfortable being himself. In his autobiography, *A Sculptor's World*, Noguchi writes about this kindergarten, "I was finally among people who seemed to take me as one of them, or rather, as somebody of interest to them. A half-breed person such as myself was a welcome addition. . . . That's why I was treated in a way, not as a freak, you might say, but somebody like themselves, or rather you might say, somebody they'd like to know."

Isamu Noguchi leans on one of his sculptures in 1985.

That hadn't been the case at his previous kindergarten, where he'd stood out because of his physical differences and also for his artistic promise. Once, he had drawn a picture of an oceanscape with sailboats, that was so good that his teachers didn't believe it was the work of a child. At Morimura, he ventured into ceramics, creating an ocean wave out of clay. With his teachers' help, he painted it blue and white, and glazed it in the kiln. For the rest of his life, Isamu would remember the seemingly magic transformation of soft clay into a sculptural blue-and-white wave. The wave was the start of Isamu's artistic career. About this time, he told his mother that he wanted to become an artist instead of a soldier. In his autobiography, he wrote that he remembered the waves from the turbulent voyage he and Leonie had taken from San Francisco to Japan.

Unfortunately, making the wave at the Morimura Kindergarten was a lone bright spot during Isamu's early years in Japan. Leonie and Isamu were left to fend for themselves in this country, where they were treated like foreigners. Leonie had a few school connections in Japan but no family. Till the end of his life, Isamu felt that his birth had been unfortunate. The dark cloud of his father's early abandonment haunted him throughout his life and reinforced his feeling that he never really belonged anywhere.

2

Like Father, Like Son

Yonejiro, or Yone, as he was sometimes called, wasn't physically present during much of his son's life. Maybe because of his absence, he wielded much power over his son. Yone's own goals and ambitions seemed to have a major influence on the choices that Isamu would make throughout his life. Even though the two never really got to know one another, they shared a sense of displacement. Both were torn between America and Japan. Like Isamu, Yone flip-flopped between the two, never really sure where he belonged. Japan gave him life—both his parents were Japanese. America, however, gave him a life purpose—it was in America where Yone came of age as a poet and artist.

Like his son would do almost 20 years later, Yone boarded a steamship on a trans-Pacific voyage in 1893. In Yone's case, the ship, called the *Belgic*, set sail from Tokyo and ended its journey in San Francisco. In the 1890s, this was already a well-worn route for Asian immigrants, who arrived daily in the largest city on the West Coast to work on the railroad or to mine the "gold fields." The discovery of gold in San Francisco in 1848 had prompted a gold rush that attracted many immigrants from China, as well as from Mexico, Chile, Ireland, Germany, and France.

By the time Yone arrived, the gold was long gone, but that didn't matter because he wasn't interested in mining or digging. He had always been fascinated by language—as a child, he slept with his spelling book beneath his pillow—and he wanted to learn English. He was also curious about America because he had heard that it offered many opportunities for a person who was driven to succeed.

When Yone arrived, he found a job delivering newspapers for the Patriotic League, a group of young Japanese political refugees. He soon found that it was difficult for him to support himself delivering newspapers, and the job didn't provide much of an opportunity to learn English, so, he quit and became a houseboy for a San Francisco family. Each day, he prepared their breakfast and dinner, and during the time in between, he studied English at an elementary school. At night, as he washed the dinner dishes, he'd recite to himself the English poems he'd learned in school. When he grew bored with elementary school, Yonejiro left his job as a houseboy, crawling out of a window in his employer's home one morning to make his way to Palo Alto. There he attended classes at Stanford University and heard about a famous poet named Joaquin Miller.

Yone had heard that Miller sometimes let students stay with him at his home in the Oakland hills, so he paid him a visit. Miller liked him right away. During the afternoons, the two worked together clearing land and planting trees and shrubs. In the mornings, Miller would write poetry, and Yone would spend hours drinking in volumes of American and English poetry. He began writing some of his own poetry in English, his adopted language. In June 1896, five of Yone's English poems were published in a literary journal. Three months later, he published his first volume of poetry, called *Seen and Unseen, or Monologues of a Homeless Snail.*

Joaquin Miller, a poet and adventurer, helped Yone Noguchi make a name for himself after his arrival in the United States.

Yone had arrived in America knowing hardly any English. Three years later, he was a published poet. The speed of his success is quite remarkable. It was due in part to his knack for introducing himself to people who could help him advance in the world of letters. Yone was not shy about apprenticing himself to people of influence. A few years later, when he traveled to England and published a small book of poems there, he sent copies to every newspaper, magazine, and famous English person he could think of—including the Queen of England and the Prince of Wales. Being associated with Joaquin Miller brought him instant recognition. He was not only Yone Noguchi, the poet. He was Yone Noguchi, apprentice of Joaquin Miller. The association brought his poems attention. So did his nationality.

In the late 1800s, America was experiencing a "Japan boom." *Japonisme*, a craze for all things Japanese, had already swept through Europe. This fad influenced painters and designers, who began to incorporate the Japanese ideals of simplicity and craftsmanship into their own work. Japanese art began showing up at international fairs, like the Philadelphia Centennial Exhibition of 1876. In the 1880s and 1890s, many Europeans and Americans traveled to Japan to find out more about this mysterious, exotic land.

In 1898, an American monthly magazine published a novella titled *Madame Butterfly*. It's the story of a *geisha*, or Japanese entertainer, who falls in love with an American naval officer. He casts her aside when he returns home to marry his American fiancée. When the story was adapted for the stage in 1900, it became widely known and very popular. *Madame Butterfly* was just one of many Japanese-influenced creations that captivated people at the turn of the twentieth century. Americans took an interest in decorating their homes with Japanese woodblock prints, ceramics, chinaware, and other bric-a-brac. The country was primed for fascination with Yone, a poet from Japan who wrote poems in English. Critics praised his poems' "Oriental character" and exotic imagery.

Once Yone established a reputation in San Francisco, he was ready to move to New York City to make a name for himself there. He rented a room on the West Side and went to work on a book called *Ocho-san's Diary*, written as a first-person account by Miss Butterfly, an outspoken young Japanese woman, about her first trip to America. (Before he published the work, he changed her name to Miss Morning Glory, perhaps because her former name was too obvious an attempt to capitalize on the success of *Madame Butterfly*.) Because Yone's English was still very poor, he posted an ad in a newspaper for an editorial assistant to help him whip the manuscript into shape. Leonie Gilmour answered his ad.

Yone was 28 years old and Leonie was 27 when they met in 1901. The two were opposites in personality. Leonie was shy, sensitive, and introverted. She had graduated from Bryn Mawr College with the dream of working as a writer or editor in New York City, but these jobs were hard to come by for a woman with no connections. In 1902, when Leonie answered Yone's newspaper ad, she was teaching Latin and French at a Catholic girls' school in Jersey City, New Jersey, and looking for extra work to earn money to pay for her mother's eye operation.

When Yone sent her the first three chapters of his book, he included a note that said, "Say, listen, can't you fix them according to your own idea? . . . This is broken English, but it got to be literature, you know, therefore I wish that you will take out some unnecessary words, and condense them nicely. Try it, please. . . . The broken English is not refined so well, so you might change as much as you please." Yone knew his prose needed a lot of work, and he seemed to be giving Leonie permission to rewrite it. She must have done a good job, because *The American Diary of a Japanese Girl* was published to rave reviews. Starting with their first collaboration, Leonie acted as his agent as well as his editor. She negotiated his publishing arrangements for *American Diary* and for the poems that he continued to write. Somewhere along the way, the nature of their relationship changed, and in 1903 they married.

It's hard to know how to characterize their relationship, because much of the correspondence that survived is businesslike in tone. In other letters Yone declared his love for several women but he never did so for Leonie, at least not in any letter that survives. Rather he seemed to look on her more as a helpmate, someone to fix his prose and sell his

Story of My Family

FROM TWO DIFFERENT WORLDS

In his autobiography, *A Sculptor's World*, Isamu Noguchi described his mother's path to America: "Her name was Leonie Gilmour. Her father, Andrew, she told me, had fled Ireland. He was an unbeliever, as was Mother. Her mother was part American-Indian and had been named Smith. Florence, her sister, had gone to California to raise goats, after working for years for the *Encyclopedia Britannica*."

About his father, Noguchi writes:

The story of my father is that of Noguchi Yonejiro, the son of a small merchant near Nagoya, who later became the poet, Yone Noguchi. As a boy he had studied in a temple, and, upon recommendation of the priest, he was sent for further studies to Tokyo. Somehow he was able to enter Keio University, and in the spirit of the time he was fired with the desire for knowledge of English and for going to America, which he did in 1893. His life in California is reflected in his early poetry, in songs to the High Sierras and Yosemite. There is also his loneliness and nostalgia for things Japanese.

He became a well-known figure among the Imagist poets of the day, in both America and England.

Following his return to Japan, my father resumed his connection with Keio University as a professor of English, a position he held until work to American publishers while he was traveling abroad. He didn't treat her with respect; in fact, he was in love with another woman even while Leonie was pregnant with Isamu. He proposed marriage to another woman even though he was still lawfully married to Leonie. In 1904, a few months before Isamu's birth, Yone abandoned Leonie and returned to Japan. Leonie moved to Los Angeles, far away from long-time friends and colleagues, who might have asked awkward

his death. He wrote many books in English on Japanese art. . . . He was like a bridge between Japan and the West, but, like others, was swept up in the nationalism of the war.

In his life, Isamu seems to follow closely in his father's footsteps. Like his father, Isamu becomes an artist of acclaim by conflating Japanese and American aesthetics. Like his father, he spends ample time in both countries. It is actually his Irish-American mother, Leonie, however, who encourages him to become an artist. Isamu doesn't have enough contact with his father during the course of his childhood for Yone to have much of a direct influence, although a sense of competition with his father is partly what drives Isamu to succeed, especially during his early career.

There is one major difference between Isamu and his father. Once Yone moves back to Japan after a few years living in America, there's no question as to which country he belongs. He comes down squarely on the side of Japan in all political matters. Isamu, however, doesn't have the luxury of being just American or just Japanese. He must waver between both lands.

Geraldine Farrar, a famed soprano, helped popularize *Madame Butterfly* and Japanese culture by playing the lead role in the Metropolitan Opera's version in 1907.

questions, to have her child. In the hospital where she gave birth, she registered as Mrs. Yone Noguchi.

With her hospital registration, she blew her cover. The name caught the attention of a reporter with the *Los Angeles Herald* whose editor apparently considered the story worthwhile, because it soon ran under the headline, "Yone Noguchi's Babe Pride of Hospital: White Wife of Author Presents Husband With Son." Yone was a celebrity, and now, so was Isamu. The article read, "That the wife of the man who had achieved so much success in the literary world should be lying sick in the hospital, surrounded only by strangers, seems strangely sad, but Noguchi, the father, is far away in Japan and knows nothing of the little son who bears his name." The reporter went on to marvel at Isamu's appearance,

> The young man gives promise of being in every way a fine specimen of the kind that is holding the attention of the whole civilized world. In spite of the fact that the baby was born under the flag of Uncle Sam and that his mother is an American woman, of the blue-eyed type, he has not a single trace of anything but Japanese and the hair and eyes are as black as his father's ever were.

Baby Noguchi was indeed a mix of many cultures. His mother's father was Scotch-Irish and her mother was part American Indian. These were cultures that couldn't have seemed more different from his father's Japanese culture.

3

Choosing Between Noguchi and Gilmour

In America, people noticed Isamu's Asian features and called him half-Japanese. In Japan, however, people remarked on the Caucasian features of the half-American boy. Isamu couldn't win, and neither, it seemed, could Yone. His initial reception in his native country was less than welcoming; it made his countrymen suspicious that he had received recognition abroad. One critic wrote of his work, "[His] fundamental feelings are so unlike those of a Japanese that one seems to be reading a Westerner's poems translated directly into our language." Yone wrote a poem called "Dual Citizen" about his troubles:

> When Japanese read my Japanese poetry they say,
> "His Japanese poems are not so good but perhaps his
>   English poems are better."
> When Westerners read my English poems, they say,
> "I can't bear to read his English poems, but his Japa-
>   nese poems must be superb."
> To tell the truth,

I have no confidence in either language.

In other words, I guess I am a dual citizen.

Isamu knew the feeling. After Leonie found out about Yone's other wife and family, she and Isamu moved out of Tokyo to the seaside village of Chigasaki, a small community of fishermen and farmers. Leonie was attracted by the sea air, surrounding hills, and picturesque groves of pine trees, but her commute was tough. She took the train to and from Yokohama each day to teach at a girls' school. That meant she was not around much to protect Isamu or to be his companion, and in Chigasaki he found little companionship among the tight-knit villagers.

Isamu may have stood out in Tokyo, but in Chigasaki, where it was even less likely that anyone had ever laid eyes on a foreigner, his differences were even more pronounced. In his elementary school picture, seven-year-old Isamu wears a shirt and pants, and his curly hair is long enough to conceal the tops of his ears. His classmates are dressed in kimonos, and they have closely shaved heads and sunburned faces from working outdoors with their fishermen and farmer fathers. Isamu recalled later in life that his classmates called him a *baka* ("dummy") and *gaijin* ("foreigner"). In his autobiography, though, he writes that by then he'd become a Japanese boy who skins willows to make whistles, fishes for eel, and delights in local festivals. He couldn't have blended in so well, though, according to his other recollections. He said in an interview shortly before he died:

I remember incidents in Chigasaki . . . myself being treated in an odd way, to my discomfort. After all, I was something of a freak, without any doubt, and children don't hide their feelings. . . . It was in the summertime that . . . my memories are keenest. Various . . . incidents of childhood trauma, of running away, of feeling abandoned, and wanting to go away, and "They'll feel sorry later on."

A small village outside Yokohama, Japan, similar to the one where Noguchi grew up.

It didn't help that, in addition to his physical differences, he was the son of a red-haired foreign woman who was raising him alone. They rented a room in a farmhouse, and the other children would tease Isamu on his way to and from school, pushing him into rice paddies, throwing stones at him, and shoving him into stacks of straw. One of his neighbors later recalled tormenting Isamu in his front yard as Leonie returned home from work. "Mrs. Leonie came bounding into the yard as fast as a rabbit," he remembered. "Without a word she grabbed Isamu, hugged him to her body, and immediately fled back to her house."

Isamu's memories of being teased in Chigasaki remained vivid his whole life. In addition, he always associated Chigasaki with an all-consuming fear that his mother wasn't coming home. Every day, he worried about it. He'd worry right up until the minute he spotted her walking home from the train station. It's no wonder he was so anxious—Leonie was all he had in the world. His moments with Leonie when she read to him from books of Greek mythology and the poems by William Blake, Chaucer, and Lady Gregory were his favorite moments. In his autobiography, he wrote, "All I remember of my earliest time is being a child with his mother; that was the total of my existence all the time I was in Japan."

Two major developments happened in Isamu's eighth year—he started going to a new, English school and he got a baby sister. Ailes was born in 1912—neither Isamu nor Ailes ever discovered the identity of her father. Leonie kept it a secret. When Isamu was eight, he didn't much care about the name of his sister's father. His main reaction to the new arrival was despair over having to share his mother with this pesky little girl. (He liked her much better later, after they had both grown up.)

As for school, Isamu had had enough of Chigasaki's. He insisted on being educated as an American boy at a Catholic school in Yokohama. He registered there as "Isamu Gilmour," not "Isamu Noguchi," as he'd been known previously. Each morning he woke up at 4:00 A.M. to catch the train to Yokohama, where he'd walk two miles to St. Joseph's. Classes there were taught in English, and his fellow students were a mix of cultures, including Indian, Filipino, and European. Even in this melting pot of cultures, among other boys who were of mixed blood, Isamu felt estranged. He wasn't teased and tormented, but he didn't feel like he fit in.

Life improved when his mother decided to build the family a house in Chigasaki, and she asked Isamu to help with the construction. Leonie hoped that Isamu would one day become an artist, like his father. He'd already declared his wish to be an artist after making the blue wave out of clay at the kindergarten in Tokyo. Reading him poetry and getting him involved in building the family's new home were Leonie's ways of prompting Isamu to start thinking about what he'd like to create. The nine-year-old surprised his mother, and the carpenters who were building the house, with his skill and sense of purpose.

Maybe because he'd been involved in its construction, he had very fond feelings for the finished home. The neighbors called it the "Triangle House," because it was three-sided, to fit into the pyramid-shaped plot of land. Isamu's favorite spot in the house was a round window on the second floor that looked westward toward Mount Fuji. He especially loved to look out that window as the sun was setting. He wrote in his autobiography, "[T]hat was my big experience which started me off into life, and part of my consciousness ever since."

TYPICAL JAPANESE BOY

In his autobiography, Isamu Noguchi wrote that by the time he was five—that is, by the time he'd spent three full years in Japan—he was a "typical Japanese boy." What did that mean in the early 1900s? What did a typical Japanese boy do? Children had no TV, Internet, or video games. Isamu gave us some clues when he wrote that by the time he was old enough to go to kindergarten, he was very aware of nature. He would look through the window of his house and see Mount Fuji. Nearby were a pine grove, potato fields, and the sea. He would sing "Yuyake, Koyake," or "Sunrise, Sunset"—a popular Japanese children's song—when he saw the sunset.

Noguchi also mentioned festivals. During his early life in Tokyo and Chigasaki, he probably saw or participated in the celebrations of many festivals, including two of the biggest:

• Obon Festival, or the Festival of the Dead, in late summer, a Buddhist event that commemorates ancestors. For three days, people hang lanterns in front of their houses to guide their ancestors' spirits. They visit graves and make food offerings, and they watch dancers perform traditional *obon* dances. At

Isamu finally made some friends during the summer of 1914. Some of the surrounding homes were vacation homes for families who came to Chigasaki in the summer. He and some of the children from those families would play together at the beach. When it was time to return to school, he went back to St. Joseph's for a little while, then stopped going altogether. Leonie wrote to a friend that Isamu insisted on staying home because he was tired of the long train journey. Isamu recalled that Leonie made the decision that she would homeschool him. Whoever made the decision, Isamu was home and under Leonie's care.

the end of the festival, people float the paper lanterns down rivers, to guide the spirits back to their own world.

• Tango-no-Sekku, or Boy's Festival, in early May, honoring the boys of Japan. (A Girl's Day is observed in March.) Traditionally, people celebrate with colorful *koinobori,* or streamers made of paper or cloth that are shaped like carp, a type of fish. The koinobori are hoisted high on tall bamboo poles. When the wind blows, they fill with air and squirm as if they were swimming through the sky. One carp is flown for each son in the family.

Isamu also wrote of the kabuki troupes who visited his town. These were traveling theater groups who performed comic plays about everyday life. Kabuki was invented in 1603 and is still performed today. The actors are characterized by their elaborate makeup and stylized movements. It's interesting that all of these things that rendered Isamu a "typical Japanese boy" would later become important when he decided to become an artist. When you reach the later chapters in this book, think back to Isamu's childhood experiences with nature, festivals, paper lanterns, fish-shaped streamers, and Kabuki troupes, and think about how his childhood informed his artistic output.

Isamu told Leonie that he had decided he wanted to be a landscape gardener, so she put him in charge of the garden at the Triangle House. He loved it. He tended rose bushes, planted pansies, hiked to nearby hills to look for mountain azaleas, and even created a brook in the garden by diverting water from the water pump. He was proud of his 50 rose bushes. Leonie took him on walks through nearby temple gardens and signed him up for fencing classes. For a full term, he was apprenticed to a carpenter and learned the basics of cabinetmaking and wood-carving. "That was," he later wrote, "the only education I remember with pleasure. All the rest of it means nothing to me. It's the only thing I remember that had some bearing on my future."

"When I was thirteen years old," Isamu wrote in his auto-biography, "my mother decided that I must go to America to continue my education. I am sure that she must have been concerned about the unfortunate situation of children of mixed blood growing up in the Japan of those days—half in and half out. She decided that I had better become completely American." Actually, according to letters Leonie wrote to a friend at home in America, Leonie was specifically concerned with the rumors she kept hearing about the boys at St. Joseph's. She had moved Ailes and Isamu to a home closer to St. Joseph's so Isamu wouldn't have a four-hour commute each day. She heard, however, that the boys at St. Joseph's were "immoral." She wrote to her friend that the school "is not good for developing character and originality." Isamu was at a crucial point in his life—Leonie recognized that around age 13 is when a boy becomes a young man, and she didn't want people influencing him negatively at this critical juncture. Also, she knew that if he was still in Japan when he turned 18, he might have to serve in the Imperial Japanese Army.

Around the same time, she read an article in *Scientific American* magazine titled "The Daniel Boone Idea in Education" about an unconventional school called the Interlaken School in Indiana, where students were encouraged to learn by doing. (Daniel

Boone, a pioneer woodsman, was born in 1734 in Pennsylvania. Boone had hardly any formal schooling. For him, the outdoors was a schoolhouse, and that's where the renowned woodsman, explorer, and hunter learned self-reliance, resourcefulness, and survival skills.) Leonie didn't want Isamu to be a woodsman, but she liked the idea of a school where students were encouraged to work with their hands in the shop and garden. She wanted Isamu in a school that allowed him space to find his own way. She wrote to Dr. Edward Rumely, the founder of the Interlaken School, and supplied Isamu's grades from St. Joseph's, which were high in drawing (90), reading (90) and penmanship (94) and mediocre in mathematics (70), geography (73), and French (53). Leonie wrote that Isamu was always at the head of his class in art. Rumely accepted Isamu and even agreed to give him a scholarship. Leonie arranged for Isamu to leave immediately in order to make it to Indiana in time to join the summer session. She booked him a spot on a steamship leaving from Tokyo on June 27, 1918.

For Isamu, his mother's decision that he should attend school in America was very quick and a great shock. As far as he was concerned, he had never lived anywhere but Japan—he had arrived as a two-year-old. Even though Japan hadn't been the easiest place to grow up, it was all he knew. Besides, he'd never been away from his mother before. He felt banished. To aggravate his anxiety, his father showed up at the boat and commanded Isamu to stay in Japan. This was the first time Yonejiro had spoken to Isamu since he was a baby, and Isamu didn't know what to do. Yonejiro and Leonie fought with one another on the dock, and when Yonejiro demanded that Isamu come back ashore, Leonie yelled, "No!" Isamu followed her lead and issued his own firm "No." He was off.

4

Isamu in America

Isamu's boat trip was exciting. He and the other passengers celebrated the Fourth of July twice, in two different time zones. His first view of America, the country where he was born, was the majestic, pine-stippled coastline of the Northwest. When the boat docked in Seattle, a representative from the YMCA was waiting to meet him. As he directed Isamu toward the next leg of his trip, he offered him a piece of Juicy Fruit gum. The 14-year-old boy had never tasted anything so delicious. He immediately felt that America must be a great place to have such a wonderful thing.

Isamu boarded a train for Chicago that was filled with soldiers headed for the war in Europe. When they saw him, all alone with a tag pinned to his shirt announcing his name and destination, they took him under their wing and made sure he had enough to drink and eat during the three-day trip. Two trains later and three weeks after he left Yokohama, Isamu arrived in Rolling Prairie, Indiana. He was the only person to get off the train.

This is the train station that greeted Noguchi when he arrived in Rolling Prairie, Indiana.

From the train stop, Isamu walked two miles to the Interlaken School, lugging his suitcase and the box of carpenters' tools he brought all the way from Japan. He was used to walking two miles to school—he'd had to do so in Yokohama—but it was the middle of July, and the summer heat was sweltering. All he could see for miles around was an endless expanse of cornfields. There were no trees to provide shade.

When Isamu arrived at the school, he saw that it consisted of a bunch of buildings spread along a lake, called Silver Lake. The buildings—all made of wood—consisted of a main building, a craft shop, a metalworking shop, a print shop, a woodworking shop, a gymnasium, and student dormitories. Because this was the summer session, the students slept in tents by the lake instead of in the log cabins that served as dormitories the rest of the year.

The director of the summer school reported to his boss on Isamu's arrival:

> I have a little Jap in camp—half Japanese, half-English. He's a peach. He was very interested in woodwork, wanted to go to the wood-shop. I send him, with flying colors. He came back to me almost in tears. "I wanted to make something that I've planned for a long time, and Mr. Hedrain [the woodworking teacher] set me to planing a block of wood, just to plane it."

Isamu was way beyond planing a block of wood. He'd helped construction workers build his mother's house after all, and he'd apprenticed with a carpenter for a full school term. The school director understood his frustration and set him up in his own corner of the studio. Isamu quickly impressed the director and his fellow students with his masterful carvings. The director wrote, "[T]he boys are already wearing a path to his door."

As at St. Joseph's, Isamu was known to the people at the Interlaken School as "Isamu Gilmour," not "Isamu Noguchi." Isamu Gilmour was off to a good start—he was the center of attention, with boys clamoring to know how he used his tools to such great effect. In the morning, he and the other boys would do manual and farm labor. Before lunch, they'd swim in the lake.

After lunch, they had lessons in science, literature, and other academic subjects. From 4:00 P.M. to 6:00 P.M., the boys could choose from horseback riding, canoeing or tennis. After dinner, they did their homework until bedtime. Isamu felt like he was a guest at a nonstop party.

All too suddenly, the party was over. All the other students went home when the summer term ended in August. Isamu stayed in one of the school buildings with two caretakers, waiting for the fall term to start. It never did as the school was taken over for wartime use. In October, Leonie received an urgent telegram in Japan that read, "SCHOOL CLOSED SEND MONEY AND ADVICE." Isamu, meanwhile, had no idea what was going on. He passed his fourteenth birthday in November alone on the empty campus, feeling utterly abandoned. The principal and teachers who'd stayed on at the school became sick with the flu, so no one was able to look after Isamu. "I had the use of a horse upon which I rode out like a cowboy at four in the morning to fetch the mail and the victuals," he later recalled, "getting back in time to make breakfast." Leonie's letters took a while to arrive, and the school's staff didn't want to send Isamu anywhere without his mother's permission. They waited for a month for word from Leonie.

Finally, Leonie's letter arrived: In it, she instructed the staff to enroll Isamu in the public high school in nearby LaPorte and to consult with the local YMCA or Boy Scout master about finding a home for him. This was all Leonie could do from so far away. In December, the summer school director's wife took him home with her and he began at the local high school in Rolling Prairie. It was Chigasaki all over again, but this time, the students harassed him because he was half-Japanese. Rolling Prairie was a tiny town, a community of farmers who probably hadn't seen many foreigners. They didn't trust the unfamiliar. Luckily, Dr. Rumely, the founder of the Interlaken School, plucked Isamu from Rolling Prairie and found him a home in LaPorte, which was a bit larger and less insular.

At LaPorte High School he was known as "Sam," and he lived with the Mack family. Charles Mack, known to the people of LaPorte as "Doc," was a church pastor. Four of his children had already grown up and moved on, but the two youngest sons remained, so Isamu was the fifth in the household. The family members welcomed Isamu, including him in their day-to-day doings. All the while, Isamu kept up a correspondence by mail with Dr. Rumely, who was in New York. Rumely freely gave Isamu advice, so much so that he and Isamu developed a mentor-protégé or a father-son relationship. Isamu's real father, Yonejiro, actually traveled quite close to LaPorte at one point while Isamu was there. Yonejiro was in Chicago for three weeks during a three-month tour of America to lecture on Japanese poetry. He was only a two-hour train ride from Isamu, yet he made no attempt to contact him. When Isamu found out, he felt angry. He decided that he disliked his father intensely. He wrote in his autobiography that he developed a "moral loathing" for his father during this time.

Dr. Rumely, on the other hand, took a great interest in Isamu's well-being. He gave him money to open a bank account and told him to keep him informed of how he was spending his money and how much he was saving. He asked Isamu to tell him about his schoolwork and his teachers. Isamu wrote to Dr. Rumely about his grades, the books he was reading, and even about his broken bicycle and the hand-me-down coat he'd acquired from a kind neighbor. Rumely encouraged Isamu by telling him that the best advantage to have in America is no advantage at all. He meant that in America, it's possible to start with nothing and become a success. "This was his greatest gift to me," Isamu said later. "And I think it's correct."

Leonie and Ailes returned to America in 1920, when Isamu was halfway through high school, but Leonie never tried to arrange a reunion. She was just scraping by in San Francisco, and she didn't have the money to travel or to send to Isamu so

This photograph of downtown LaPorte, Indiana, was taken in 1914. Isamu Noguchi went to high school in this Indiana town.

that he could travel. She felt that he was in good hands with Dr. Rumely.

Leonie didn't make it to Isamu's graduation from LaPorte High School, but he still had a crowd cheering him on that day—June 7, 1922, four years, almost to the day, after he'd arrived in America. He made Dr. Rumely proud with his high grades—95 in art, 97 in chemistry, 96 in math, 96 in biology and 93 in physics. He'd also designed the cover of the yearbook—a drawing of two Grecian-style male nudes and a triangular stone tablet that read "1922." In the yearbook, he had no activities listed next to his name. He'd been busy after school delivering newspapers on weekdays and working part-time jobs on the weekends to earn spending money. Also, he'd never tried to fit in with the crowd at school—maybe because he already had experienced how awful it feels to be rejected by the crowd. He said later, "I did not have intimate friends, excepting for the Rumelys and the Macks. . . . Those people were my friends and they helped me."

After his graduation, Dr. Rumely asked Isamu what he wanted to be, and without hesitation Isamu said, "An artist." He wasn't really sure what he wanted to do, but Leonie had told him from the time he was a baby that becoming an artist was her dream for him, so this was the answer on the tip of his tongue. He admired the work of French sculptor Auguste Rodin, and he thought he might like to be a sculptor.

ISAMU'S MENTORS

Isamu Noguchi had a knack for cultivating mentor–protégé relationships with a series of individuals who offered him fatherly advice and showed him the care and concern that his father did not give him. The following are Noguchi's primary mentors:

• **Dr. Edward Rumely (1882–1964):** The founder of the Interlaken School that Isamu traveled to America to attend at age 13. Dr. Rumely "rescued" Isamu when he was stranded with nowhere to go at the closing of the school. Rumely found a family in LaPorte, Indiana, that was willing to take him in; enrolled him in the public high school; and kept close track of his progress. It was Dr. Rumely's idea for Isamu to attend medical school, but his mentor's support did not end when Isamu decided to pursue a career in art instead. In fact, he helped Noguchi with the rent for his first sculpture studio and secured him commissions from friends.

• **Onorio Ruotolo (1888–1966):** In 1923, Ruotolo founded the Leonardo da Vinci School of Art on Manhattan's Lower East

Dr. Rumely had a different occupation in mind, however. He knew that Isamu's science grades were good enough to get him into medical school. Rumely interpreted Isamu's dexterity with his carpenters' tools as evidence that he'd be a terrific surgeon. He knew that if Isamu became a doctor, he'd have a stable and prosperous life. Still, he didn't discourage his artistic ambition. Rumely arranged for Isamu to apprentice to a friend, a sculptor, Gutzon Borglum, the artist who would later carve the gigantic likenesses of George Washington, Thomas Jefferson, Abraham Lincoln and Theodore Roosevelt on the face of Mount Rushmore. Borglum was at home in Connecticut and working that summer on a commission from the city of Newark, New Jersey: a Civil War memorial composed of more than 40 figures, including horses.

Side. He learned to sculpt at the Royal Academy of Fine Arts in Naples, Italy, and he was well-known for his skill in making portrait busts. He was steeped in the academic style of sculpting, and that's what he taught Isamu Noguchi when he started coming to his school in 1924. Noguchi's discovery of abstract art created a rift between him and his first art mentor, but Ruotolo's influence stuck, because to fund his travels, Noguchi continued to make portrait busts throughout much of his career.

• R. Buckminster Fuller (1895–1983): It's hard to know where to start with Buckminster Fuller—he was many things, including an inventor, engineer, architect, philosopher, and writer, but most of all, he was one of the most inventive thinkers of the twentieth century. He received 28 patents in his lifetime, and he authored 28 books and received 47 honorary doctorates. Even Albert Einstein once said to him, "Young man, you amaze me!" Fuller and Noguchi became friends when he sat for one of Noguchi's portrait busts. Noguchi cast Fuller's bust in shiny chrome, an appropriate material for a portrait of a man who was always thinking into the future.

Gutzon Borglum, an American sculptor best known for carving Mount Rushmore, allowed Noguchi to work for him when he graduated from high school.

When Isamu arrived in Connecticut, he saw that the commission was a complex operation with models and actual horses posing while Borglum sculpted. Also on-site were Italian plasterers and metal casters who assisted Borglum. Isamu's job was to pose as a model for General Sherman and to force the horses to hold difficult poses with their mouths open and legs up in the air. He also chopped firewood and tutored Borglum's 10-year-old son for his salary of five dollars a week. Borglum was the opposite of Rumely—he seemed not to want to teach Isamu anything at all. Isamu was more an errand boy than an apprentice. Anything he learned that summer was from his own efforts to observe the plasterers, the casters, and Borglum at work. He made use of his observations to make a bust of Abraham Lincoln. At the end of the summer, however, Borglum destroyed any feeling of progress or success Isamu may have gained by announcing to him that he would never be a sculptor.

5

The Road to Artist

After his unfortunate apprenticeship with Borglum, Isamu went to New York City and stayed with Dr. Rumely's family at their Manhattan apartment. He had a big decision to make—whether he would pursue art, as his mother had always wanted, or medicine, which Dr. Rumely seemed to be pushing. He'd been interested in art since he was in kindergarten and, despite what Borglum declared, he seemed to have an aptitude for it. Dr. Rumely's influence was strong, though, and he made a good point that medicine would provide a stable income. Isamu took Dr. Rumely's advice and enrolled in the premedical program at Columbia University in February 1923. When Leonie found out, she was very upset—upset enough to move from San Francisco to the East Coast.

When she arrived in New York, she visited Dr. Rumely and scolded him for convincing Isamu to pursue a career in medicine. In a letter to a friend, she described condemning the doctor for "turning a boy of artistic temperament toward a career for which he was entirely unsuited." Isamu was caught between his mother and Dr. Rumely. The latter had been his guardian and confidant for the last five years. He'd left Leonie when he was 14, and he was now a grown-up 19-year-old. He'd learned to be independent, but he was still unsure about what to do with his life. Being lobbed back and forth like a Ping-Pong ball between his mother's desires to Dr. Rumely's didn't help him with his confusion. What were his own ambitions? Forget about the others—what did *he* want to do?

One thing he knew was that he resented his mother butting in to his life. He still felt that she'd abandoned him by sending him to America. She couldn't show up after all these years and impose her will. Besides, he'd become accustomed to being free and independent. He chafed under her attempts to tell him what to do. He moved in with her and Ailes briefly, but after three months he left and rented his own apartment in Greenwich Village. He took classes at Columbia during the day and washed dishes at night to pay for his apartment and to earn spending money. He was unhappy—he hated the premed classes, but he didn't have enough confidence in his artistic talents to pursue that path.

He didn't make any friends at Columbia, but he made a few friends outside of school. One was Michio Ito, who was from a family well-known in the Japanese theater world. Ito was a dancer who had moved to New York after living in Paris and London. His choreography incorporated elements from many cultures—including Brazilian tango and Japanese sword-dancing. He had much influence on American dance, which was, at that time, still mostly European-style ballet. When Isamu met him, Ito ran his own dance studio and choreographed Broadway shows. He was a model for Isamu. Ito was Japanese, and he was thriving in New York by creating art that blended elements from different cultures. No one was calling him a "freak," the label Isamu had become used to, from living in small towns like Chigasaki and Rolling Prairie. In fact, Ito,

Michio Ito, a Japanese dancer shown here in costume in 1916, befriended and inspired Noguchi.

who was 31 years old at the time, was very successful—and he had a following of beautiful young women. He showed Isamu what was possible.

One day Leonie was walking around the Lower East Side when she noticed an art school housed in a former church on

Avenue A called The Leonardo da Vinci Art School. It was a brand-new school founded by local Italian-American community leaders to teach their children the arts and crafts of their homeland—and to keep them busy and out of trouble. Classes were conducted at night, and tuition was free. Leonie thought it might be a good place for Isamu to go and test out his sculpting abilities. It was close to his apartment, and the price was right.

Isamu went and looked around the school. He met the director, Onorio Ruotolo, who urged him on the spot to try sculpting something. Isamu copied a plaster model of a foot in clay, and as soon as Ruotolo saw it, he admitted Isamu into the school. Isamu attended art classes at night and premedical classes during the day. Ruotolo recognized his great talent. He taught Isamu basic sculpture techniques that he used for his own work. Isamu learned fast. After only three months, he had created enough pieces to have a show. The August 24, 1924, edition of *The World and Word* ran a photo of Isamu surrounded by 4 of the 21 pieces on display, with a headline that read: "19-Year-Old Japanese American Boy Shows Marked Ability as a Sculptor."

Isamu's sculptures were of classical subjects, including Christ, the biblical figure Salome, a fountain, and an archer. They were sculpted in the academic style—the focus was on figurative, or symbolic, subjects from mythology and ancient times who were models of perfection. Academic sculptors strove to faithfully re-create their subjects' physicality, down to details such as muscles and the way the skin stretches over the bones. (Academic painters strove to find the perfect shade of pink to paint a realistic flesh tone.) Whether they were sculpting a mythological figure or a bust of the person sitting right in front of them, they prized the ability to be able to portray a person expressing some emotion. *The World and Word* reporter mentioned that Isamu was the son of Yone Noguchi, and he gave him a great review, writing that the sculpture of Christ appeared to be feeling "a sorrow more than divine." Noguchi was elected to the National Sculpture Society.

About that time, the New York art world was experiencing a major shift. Modern art had established itself among the more progressive artists and galleries in the city. Modernism was a backlash to academic styles of art like the one Ruotolo taught. Modern artists painted what they called "realist" subjects, such as people drinking at saloons or street musicians or workers toiling away in sweatshops. Instead of portraying mythological and biblical figures, they were inspired by modern, gritty scenes of city living. Modernists also painted and sculpted abstract concepts that were even further from academic art.

Ruotolo rejected modernism outright, but Isamu was excited by the possibilities presented by these new modes of expression. He and Ruotolo fought about academicism versus modernism, and finally Ruotolo kicked Isamu out of his studio. Isamu rented his own studio elsewhere in Greenwich Village and received his first commissions to make portrait busts. The commissions came from Dr. Rumely and his friends.

Isamu continued to create works in the academic style in which he'd been taught, but he frequented galleries that displayed modern art, such as J.B. Neumann's New Art Circle and Alfred Stieglitz's An American Place. Seeing these other artists' unique work was frustrating, because he hadn't found a style of his own. While he was making a portrait bust of Michio Ito, the dancer told Isamu all about his days in Paris. These stories inspired Isamu to apply for a Guggenheim Fellowship that would pay for him to study abroad for two years. He was also encouraged to apply by a member of the Guggenheim family who had seen his work.

Applicants for the Guggenheim Fellowship were supposed to be between the ages of 25 and 35. Isamu was only 22, but he was one of the three artists selected for the competitive fellowship. On his application he wrote that he wanted to spend the first year of the fellowship in Paris, "studying stone and wood cutting and gaining a better understanding of the human figure." In the second and third years, he hoped to go to Asia,

MODERN ART

In Paris, France, in 1874, a group called the Anonymous Society of Painters, Sculptors, and Printmakers organized an exhibit in Paris that created quite a stir in the art world. The artists who exhibited their work in this show had been rejected by the Académie des Beaux-Arts, a prestigious art institution in Paris that prized formal and rigid styles of painting. The Anonymous artists were the first practitioners of impressionism, the earliest modern art movement. Impressionists preferred to paint outside, so they could study light and its effect on objects. They painted landscapes and scenes from daily life, unlike academy painters, whose subjects were more likely to be historic scenes from the Bible or Greek mythology, and formal portraits of aristocrats and royalty. Some well-known impressionists include Edouard Manet, Claude Monet, Edgar Degas, Pierre-Auguste Renoir, and Vincent van Gogh.

Fauvists and expressionists took modern art a bit farther away from realism by using bold, wild colors not found in nature. The first fauvist exhibition took place in 1905, a year after Isamu Noguchi was born. Fauvism was followed by cubism, which presented fragmented views of people and objects as assemblages of geometric forms. Cubists Pablo Picasso and Georges Braque were inspired by the angular shapes in African art, and they rejected the idea that art should copy nature. Still, the images in their paintings were recognizable as people, guitars, playing cards, and so on, until the later years of cubism, about 1910, when their works became entirely abstract.

The next group, the surrealists, painted what they saw in their dreams. Surrealism had a literary aspect to it—the artists practiced "automatic writing," which means they'd write spontaneously, without planning or plotting, in order to spill what lay deep in their minds, in their subconscious, onto the paper. Some famous surrealists are Salvador Dali and Marcel DuChamp. This movement lasted in Paris until World War II began brewing in the late 1930s, and many of the artists escaped to New York.

specifically to India, China, and Japan. He wrote, "I feel a great attachment to [the Orient], having spent half my life there. My father, Yone Noguchi, is Japanese and has long been known as an interpreter of the East to the West, through poetry. I wish to do the same with sculpture." He finished with a question, "May I request your assistance in enabling me to fulfill my heritage?" The choice of artist versus doctor was no longer in question— Isamu had chosen the life of an artist.

In the blank for "name" on the fellowship application, he had entered "Isamu Noguchi," and that was the name he'd keep from that point on. No more "Isamu Gilmour," as he'd been known since he was eight years old. He decided to take his Japanese surname for several reasons. For one, he felt that his artistic sensibilities had been formed while he was in Japan. Also, he intended as an artist to explore his Japanese heritage. Finally, it can't be ignored that Noguchi was his father's name. Isamu was following in his father's footsteps and adopting his father's goal—to fuse and to conquer America's and Japan's art worlds. Though Isamu disliked his father, he also seemed to want to mimic him. Maybe he wanted to prove to Yone that he was good enough. Maybe he wanted to make Yone take notice of the son he'd neglected since birth. When asked later in life about what inspired him to create art, Isamu said, "There are many emotions that get you going. One of them is anger, one of them is the desire for creativity. It's out of despair and conflict. . . . Conflict is then the spark of creation."

6

World Traveler

World War I ended in 1918, and Europeans reacted to the horrors and the death they'd witnessed during the war by giving birth to new movements in art, literature, dance, music and theater. In the 1920s, Paris was the center of this postwar renaissance. Artists from all over the world came to live there. Isamu Noguchi arrived in April 1927. He blended naturally into the vibrant community. The day after his arrival, he was already acting like a native Parisian, sipping coffee at a famous café on the Left Bank, the Greenwich Village of Paris. On his third day, he snagged an apprenticeship with the Romanian sculptor Constantin Brancusi, whose work he'd admired just a few months earlier at the Brummer gallery in New York. He later recalled, "I was transfixed by his vision."

Brancusi had studied in Paris and worked under Auguste Rodin, the sculptor whose work had prompted Isamu to seek a sculpture apprenticeship after high school. Brancusi hadn't stayed with Rodin for very long, though, because, as he once said, "Nothing grows under big trees." He did find his own style, one of abstraction that was far from Rodin's naturalist style. In a 1913 show, his abstract sculptures prompted a lot of buzz in the art world. One piece that attracted attention was *The Kiss*, a portrayal of a man and woman locked in an embrace. The blocky sculpture is carved from a single rectangular piece of stone. It looks more like a relief than what is traditionally called sculpture. Another, *Bird in Space*, is an abstract interpretation of a bird's grace and lightness. Brancusi made several versions from different materials. Each is a slender, vertical, propeller-like form that stretches toward the sky.

An acquaintance in Paris brought Isamu to Brancusi's studio, which was located near the Left Bank, in a building that from the outside looked like a warehouse. The nondescript exterior made the inside of the studio all the more surprising. The artist Man Ray said about Brancusi's studio, "I was more impressed than in any cathedral. I was overwhelmed by its whiteness and lightness." When Isamu met him, Brancusi, 51, was wearing a white smock. His hair and beard were partly white, and his two pet dogs were white. "The whole studio itself felt pure white," Isamu later wrote. "I felt the greatness of Brancusi's art the moment I stepped into his studio."

Even though Brancusi didn't hire assistants—he believed that an artist should do everything himself, including his own chores—Isamu somehow talked his way into assisting the artist. Working together was difficult, because Brancusi spoke no English and Isamu only spoke a small amount of French. They communicated through gestures. Isamu was only experienced with working with clay, so Brancusi taught him how to work with different kinds of stone and marble. Each of his tools was hung neatly on a wall, almost as carefully as if they were on display at a museum. Brancusi would select a tool for each specific task and show Isamu how to hold it and how to manage the material. Isamu noticed that Brancusi's respect for his tools and materials was similar to the sensibilities of the Japanese carpenters he'd worked with as a child. "Brancusi, like the

Three sculptures by Constantin Brancusi are shown in the above photo. From left to right are *The Sorceress*; *The Muse*; and *King of Kings*.

Japanese," he said later in his autobiography, "would take the quintessence of nature and distill it. [He] showed me the truth of the materials and taught me never to decorate or paste unnatural materials onto my sculpture, to keep them undecorated like the Japanese house."

He spent seven months as Brancusi's assistant, and the older artist's vision taught him several things that stayed with him throughout his career. The first was to be in the moment. "Never do anything as preparation for something later," he told Noguchi, "for you will never do anything better than what you do now." Another was to appreciate the material—Isamu learned to "listen" to the materials in order to know what form they should take. Also, Brancusi was a very hard worker—he lived for his art, hardly doing anything else except for seeing a movie every now and then. At that point in Isamu's life, he wasn't ready to live for his art—especially not while he was in Paris, an exciting city full of other young and social people who were also interested in art.

Isamu made friends with several painters and sculptors who later became famous, including a fellow American named Alexander Calder. Michio Ito had given him several letters of introduction to meet a number of French sculptors, but because Isamu didn't speak French, he didn't socialize with them much. Instead of going to Asia, as he had planned, Isamu stayed in Paris during the second year of his fellowship. Brancusi's influence on him had been strong, and he found himself having trouble forging his own path away from Brancusi's style.

When Isamu returned to New York, he had a show. Many of the sculptures he displayed were obviously influenced by Brancusi. The reviewers liked the work, but he didn't sell anything. Money was tight—he was trying to make enough money to give to Leonie and to his little sister, Ailes. So, he went back to making portrait busts, or "heads." This was something Isamu knew he was good at. Heads were in demand, and Isamu could—and did—make five at a time. "There was nothing to do but make heads," he wrote. "It was a matter of eating." Making heads also provided a great opportunity to get to know the people he was sculpting, because they needed to sit for him while he sculpted their likeness. Many of his sitters later became famous. He met another mentor this way—Buckminster Fuller, an inventor, engineer, architect, and philosopher. To express Fuller's futuristic, forward-thinking mind-set, Isamu crafted his bust out of shiny chrome.

Fuller wrote the introduction to Isamu's autobiography, *A Sculptor's World*. He wrote, "I first met Noguchi when I was thirty-two years old, and I recall his stated envy of the natives of various lands who seemed to 'belong' to their respective lands. As with all human beings, he had the deep yearning for the security of 'belonging'—if possible to a strong culture or at least some identifiable group."

Isamu had yet to feel that he belonged anywhere. He also felt like he was stuck in an artistic rut. In Paris, he'd learned much from Brancusi, but the sculptor's influence and vision were so strong that he was having trouble finding his own style. In fact, at the peak of his career, when an artist called him asking to be his apprentice, he'd advised the young artist not to seek out a mentor. "Yes, I [apprenticed under Brancusi]," he is quoted as saying in Sam Hunter's biography. "Because of it, it has taken me 20 years to break away from his style. If you are interested in becoming an artist, don't work with artists; work with craftsmen. Learn their techniques, but the ideas must come from you."

Besides feeling smothered by Brancusi's style, Noguchi needed to make money. With all the time he spent making portrait busts—and he was very busy with commissions—he had no time to pursue his aspirations to create modern art. He thought that if he went back to Japan and looked at the country through the eyes of an artist, he might be able to rediscover the bits and pieces of experiences he remembered from his childhood—the paper shoji screens, the garden at the Triangle House, paper origami, the temple gardens. These things were buried in his memory, and he wanted to go and see them again, because he knew that they were important to his art. He also hoped to reconcile with his father.

Once he had enough money, he embarked on his journey, stopping in Paris first to collect his tools. He spent two months in Paris, waiting for a visa that would allow him to travel to Asia. While he was there, he heard from Leonie that Yonejiro did not want him using the name "Noguchi" while he was in Japan. Once again, Yone had rejected his son. Isamu was shocked, but he continued with his original plan and set off for Asia. His first stop would be Peking, China.

Isamu stayed in Peking for six months. It was nicknamed the "Paris of the Orient," but it was actually much more affordable than Paris. Isamu was able to rent an entire house that came with a cook, a houseboy, and a rickshaw man. He studied Chinese in

PARIS IN THE 1920s

World War I raged for four years, killing 300,000 French troops alone. When it finally ended in 1918, people couldn't wait to erase the horrible memories of blood and violence—and what better way to do this than to make art, listen to music, dance, hang out at cafés, and have fun? This is exactly what happened, and it all happened in Paris. Poet Ezra Pound called the city the center of the world, and he said it was the place for people who had "cast off sanctified stupidities and timidities," in other words, people whose minds were open to new experiences. All forms of art were subject to experimentation. The city was abuzz with young artists, writers, and musicians, who exchanged ideas over tables in cafés and bars. During that time, there was a radical break with tradition. Out with the old, they said, and in with new movements in art, including cubism, surrealism, futurism and dadaism.

The artists who came before this generation had painted with the goal of faithfully recreating an image down to the color of the sitter's flesh and the details of the folds in his or her cloak. These new artists, however, were interested in symbols, concepts, and abstract interpretations of reality. They played with staid notions of art. One artist, a friend of Noguchi's named Marcel DuChamp, displayed a urinal and called it art. Noguchi never went that far, but the modern sensibilities of his Paris peers did rub off on him. He created his first abstractions in Paris in 1927.

the mornings and visited art and antique shops in the afternoon. Isamu met and studied with a renowned ink-brush painter named Ch'i Pai-shih. He created his own ink-brush paintings at home—the rickshaw man would go out to the street and bring people back to the house to sit for Noguchi.

In January, 1931, he left China and boarded a boat to Japan. Also on-board was a Japanese reporter who'd learned that Isamu was Yone Noguchi's son. The reporter made contact with his newspaper's office. While Isamu was en route, a story about him appeared in a Japanese newspaper. The headline read, "Yearning for His Father the Poet." It quoted Isamu as saying, "I remember my father's face very well. I never forgot him for a moment and I always talked about him with my mother. I never got out of my head the idea of going to Japan, where my father was, and now I am finally realizing my hopes." If Isamu was aiming for a low-pressure reconciliation, those expectations were dashed when his boat was received in Tokyo by a crowd of reporters hoping to witness a father-son reunion. Isamu tried his best to clear up the situation. He told them, "I have come to Japan not as the son of the poet Yone Noguchi. I have come as the American Isamu Noguchi to see Japan for my own sculpture. . . . I have come to Japan only for work. I will not meet my father."

On the same day, a group of reporters showed up at Yone's house. Yone told the group that he really wanted to see Isamu and that he didn't even know he was coming to Japan until he'd read the article in the newspaper. He was lying, of course. Leonie had written to him months before, and he'd told her to tell Isamu not to use his name. Obviously he'd been caught being a bad father by the local press, and he was trying to save face.

A few days later, Yone and Isamu had a tense, awkward meeting at a hotel. "I felt pity and resentment," Isamu later recalled. Yone told Isamu that his wife wasn't happy about Isamu returning to Japan. She didn't want her family tainted by scandal. Yonejiro's brother—Isamu's uncle—and other relatives welcomed him with open arms, but his father remained reserved. For the rest of Isamu's time there, they didn't communicate much.

Isamu stayed with his uncle for several months in Tokyo, but he became bored with the pampered life he was leading in the city. He felt like he wasn't working hard enough and that he wasn't progressing on his journey. He left Tokyo for Kyoto and rented a ditch digger's cottage near the enormous kiln used by Jinmatsu Uno, a well-known potter, and his son, a tile maker. He liked how silent Kyoto was as compared to Tokyo. He felt like

Buckminster Fuller, an inventor and architect, became one of Noguchi's many mentors.

he'd found a refuge, a place where he could think about his art. At the Kyoto Imperial Art Museum, he became fascinated by *haniwa*, hollow, unglazed earthenware cylinders and figurines that were placed around the tombs of Japanese rulers. He noted how modern these ancient objects seemed in style. They made him realize that sculpture had played an integral part in the lives of humans since ancient times. Before sculptures became art objects to be displayed in museums, they acted as everyday objects that held great meaning.

Walking around the temple gardens in Kyoto, he fell even more in love with Japanese culture. In his mind, the gardens were linked with the gardens Leonie would take him to see as a child and with the garden he planted at their Chigasaki house. When he left Japan in September, he was very satisfied with his trip. He hadn't really reconciled with his father, but he had grown less resentful of him. He wrote to Yone after he'd returned to America, "I wish to tell you I have no regrets about my trip to Japan. I believe it to have been all for the best. . . . I feel great attachment to Japan. I love it as much as I would some person for its faults as well as its virtues. [I] feel there is a great humanity—the foundations of my earliest dreams."

7

Turning Outward

In New York, Isamu Noguchi exhibited the ink-brush paintings and sculptures he'd made during his time in China and Japan. The critics raved about his work. The *New York Times* reviewer called his terra-cotta sculptures and busts "compellingly beautiful." Of the paintings and drawings, the same reviewer said, "There is in them something universal and eternal." One critic pointed out that there were no vestiges of Brancusi in Isamu's new work. Noguchi had found his own style. Another critic praised him for successfully combining the virtues of his double artistic heritage.

A collection of these works went on tour, to Chicago and the West Coast. Still, few of them sold. Two museums bought portrait busts for their permanent collections, but no one seemed as interested in Noguchi's more modern work. The trip to Asia had absorbed all of Isamu's funds, and with no money from these shows, he was in bad shape financially. While he was at the show opening in Chicago, he was evicted from his New York studio. He found a place to live when he returned,

Noguchi's sculpture *Walking Void* and drawing on rice paper titled *Peking Scroll* are displayed in this photograph.

but he was forced to continue churning out portrait busts to make a living.

Through the 1930s, America was suffering through the Great Depression, an economic crisis that started with the collapse of the stock market in 1929. Millions of people lost their jobs, and it was a time of great poverty and hardship. At that time, Noguchi was becoming more engaged with what was going on in the world around him. His art was about his own life, but the works were also about society's ills. In 1932, he exhibited

THE GREAT DEPRESSION

On Black Tuesday, October 29, 1929, the stock market crashed, bringing an abrupt end to the Roaring Twenties. Banks closed, businesses failed, and more than 15 million Americans became unemployed. Many Americans suffered from depression and anxiety over not being able to provide for their families. The suicide rate shot skyward. Herbert Hoover was the president of the United States when the economic crisis hit, and he sorely underestimated the situation, declaring that it would end in 60 days. The Great Depression spread outside of the United States to the rest of the world, however, and lasted through the next decade. Hoover also did not believe that the government should offer relief to the jobless, so when Franklin Delano Roosevelt, a believer in federal relief, ran against him in 1932, he was elected by a landslide.

Roosevelt offered Americans a New Deal, essentially a roster of programs that created employment that served the public good, upped the nation's general self-esteem, and provided much-needed income. He initiated these programs immediately, during his first 100 days in office. The Civil Works Administration (CWA) handed out jobs building and repairing roads, parks, airports, and other government-owned entities. People who worked for the Civilian Conservation Corps (CCC) maintained and restored

Miss Expanding Universe, his first truly abstract work. He said it expressed his love for his current girlfriend, a dancer named Ruth Page, as well as his desire to lift America's spirit during the Depression. In 1933, he exhibited a life-sized metal sculpture, *Death*, portraying a lynched man hanging from a gallows with a rope around his neck. The piece was a comment on the lynching of African Americans, a topic he'd read about in a magazine.

Isamu also happened to have death on his mind because of his mother's recent passing. In December of that year, Leonie

forests, parks, and beaches. The Farm Security Administration (FSA) provided relief for farmers and housing for migrant workers. Roosevelt's New Deal was nicknamed Alphabet Soup because of all the acronyms.

President Roosevelt didn't forget about the artists. In 1935, his administration launched the Works Progress Administration, which, by 1936, had 45,000 artists, writers, actors, and musicians on a weekly payroll. Artists who worked for the WPA's Federal Art Project were hired to create murals, paintings, and sculptures for public spaces. There were also divisions for stained glass, posters, and graphic arts, as well as a team of researchers who compiled an index of American Design. These programs put the government's money where its mouth was when it claimed that it saw art as a social and educational force, and as an integral part of society.

The WPA provided a living for many artists who later became famous, including Jackson Pollock, Mark Rothko, and Philip Guston. Unfortunately the New York office turned down all of Isamu Noguchi's proposals. He traced the rejections back to a previous encounter with the New York director, whose portrait bust he'd once made. "[S]he was sort of ugly as a mud fence," he recalled in his autobiography, "and I guess I made her even more so."

died from a severe strain of pneumonia. On New Year's Day 1934, Isamu and Ailes went to a Japanese restaurant to eat New Year cakes in memory of their mother, who loved Japan. At her gravesite, Isamu placed a haniwa he'd made in Kyoto, so she wouldn't be lonely.

During the Depression, the government created relief programs to provide jobs for the unemployed. One of these programs was the Public Works of Art Project (PWAP), which provided funding for projects that were approved by PWAP officials. Noguchi sent them a proposal for a work called *Monument to the American Plow* that consisted of tilled soil in a pyramidal shape, and at its peak was a stainless steel sculpture that represented a plow. Like many of the works he made around this time, the piece would be abstract and socially relevant. It also had both personal and universal meaning. By focusing on the plow—a truly American symbol—Noguchi hoped to celebrate American's settlers and also to express his own wish to belong to America. Unfortunately, the PWAP office turned down the project.

A few days later he submitted another project called *Play Mountain*, a playground for Central Park in New York City. The playground consisted of many pyramidal structures, providing slopes for children to sled down in the winter and fill with water to splash down in the summer. Obviously Noguchi was tired of making heads. These progressive ideas showed that he was very interested in exploring new types of art, including sculpture formed from the earth and sculpture that did more than just please the eyes. He saw *Play Mountain* as a sculpture that people, namely children, could interact with and inhabit on sunny summer and winter afternoons. "I [had] a desire to get into another realm, another dimension," he said. "[M]y head felt as though it was burning and all kinds of grand schemes came bubbling up."

Noguchi was ahead of his time. Three decades later, an "earth art" movement would embrace these ideas. For now,

In 1938, Noguchi won first prize in a national competition to design a large bronze panel to be placed over the entrance of the Associated Press building in New York City's Rockefeller Center.

though, people didn't understand Noguchi, and, as often happens with people who are ahead of their time, Noguchi was met with rejection. One member of the PWAP committee, Noguchi recalled, "laughed his head off and more or less threw us out." This series of rejections was hard to take. So was some of the criticism Noguchi received when he exhibited drawings of these pieces along with *Death* and *Miss Expanding Universe* in a solo show in New York. While reviewing the show, Henry McBride, a critic for the *New York Sun*, wrote of Noguchi, "Once an Oriental, always an Oriental." He was suspicious of Noguchi's motives in creating pro-American works like *Monument to the American Plow.* "All the time he has been over here," wrote McBride, "he has been studying our weaknesses with a view of becoming irresistible to us."

McBride's cynicism stemmed from his assumptions about Noguchi's ties with New York society. The artist had been making portrait busts for rich and influential New Yorkers for a few years, and that had led people to brand him an opportunist, or someone who is trying to get ahead by pandering to rich patrons. Of course, none of this was true and Noguchi took great offense. For the rest of his life, he abhorred art critics. "I determined to have no further truck with either galleries or critics," he wrote in his autobiography.

In fact, Noguchi had become disillusioned with the rich society people McBride accused him of admiring. After being evicted from his studio, his friends helped him find a place at the posh Hotel Des Artistes. The combination of these surroundings compared with his growing social conscience resulted in discomfort. "These contrasts of poverty and luxury made me more and more conscious of social injustice," he wrote.

In the summer of 1935, he took off for Hollywood. He'd been granted a short-term fellowship to go to Mexico to explore the burgeoning art scene there. He raised some more money for the trip by making portrait busts in California, and then he headed south of the border. Mexico had experienced a revolution and civil war in the first decade of the 1900s, and the government was now encouraging artists to create murals in order to educate the public about the country's history and its new ideals. Much of the public couldn't read, but they could interpret stories told through pictures. Isamu was so enamored by the idea of artists working for the common good that he stayed in Mexico for a year. He wrote about the experience in an article for *Art Front* magazine in 1936: "Let us make sculpture that deals with today's problems. . . . It is my opinion that sculptors, as well as painters, should not forever be concerned with pure art or meaningful

Mexican artist Diego Rivera, pictured with his wife, artist Frida Kahlo, taught Noguchi how to work in a three-dimensional style.

art, but should inject their knowledge of form and matter into the everyday, usable designs of industry and commerce."

In Mexico, Noguchi worked with famous artist Diego Rivera, and completed a mural called *History Mexico* on the wall of the Abelardo Rodriguez Market, in downtown Mexico City. The 6-foot-high (1.8 meters) and 72-foot-long (22 meters) mural is very intense and heavy-handed. It's packed with meaningful symbolism, from a Nazi swastika crushing workers' bodies to a huge fist raised in protest. During the day, Noguchi and the other artists working in Mexico City would toil on their murals. At night, there was a vibrant social scene with gatherings at Rivera's house and parties. Noguchi became close with Frida Kahlo, another renowned artist and Diego Rivera's wife. When Rivera found that they were having an affair, he chased Noguchi out of the house and up an orange tree. "Next time I see you," he warned Noguchi, waving his pistol, "I'm going to shoot you." Luckily Noguchi left Mexico without running into Rivera again.

8

Nisei

The morning of Sunday, December 7, 1941, Isamu Noguchi was driving his car from Los Angeles to buy materials at a stone supplier near San Diego. He was listening to the radio when an emergency broadcast broke through and an announcer reported, "The Japanese have attacked Pearl Harbor." This is how Noguchi learned that a war had begun between his mother's land and his father's.

A world war had been brewing since 1939, when Germany began attacking countries in Europe, including France, Poland, and Great Britain, in an attempt to build a German empire. Japan was doing the same in their part of the world, attacking nearby countries specifically to attain natural resources, including oil, which their own country was lacking. They were in the middle of a bloody war with China over control of Manchuria, called the Second Sino-Japanese War. Franklin D. Roosevelt, president of the United States, was sending supplies to countries that were being attacked by the power-hungry Germany and Japan in order to help halt their expansion. The United States also imposed an oil embargo on Japan, in an effort to persuade its leaders to stop their military campaigns. Meanwhile, Japan and Germany gained strength by forming an alliance with each other and with Italy in 1941.

Tension was rising, and President Roosevelt continued to attempt to work things out peacefully with Japan. He proposed that America would consider resuming trade with Japan if Japan would back off from China. Japan wouldn't comply with all the United States' demands, however. War was beginning to seem inevitable, so the United States beefed up its naval fleet at Pearl Harbor, a base in the Pacific Ocean off of Oahu, Hawaii. Japan saw this move as a threat to its plans to grab oil from nearby Southeast Asia. It attacked Pearl Harbor in order to cripple the American fleet that was a direct threat to its intended expansion.

America was stunned by the attack. No foreign country had ever attacked the United States on American soil. For years, Americans had heard of Japan's brutality toward China, and there were rumors that Japan was planning to follow up the December 7 sneak attack with another. Americans feared that this time Japan would attack the mainland. All of their fear and anger manifested itself as prejudice toward the Japanese Americans living among them on the West Coast.

At the time, foreign-born Asians were forbidden by law to naturalize, or become American citizens. Once President Roosevelt declared war on Japan on December 8, the group of Japanese-American immigrants who were born in Japan, called *issei,* were considered "enemy aliens." Their sons and daughters, the second-generation immigrants who had been born in America, or *nisei,* were full-fledged Americans, but the general public still saw them as enemies who were somehow collaborating with Japan. In the days after the attack, the authorities rounded up prominent Japanese Americans, including community leaders, newspaper editors, priests, even Noguchi's old friend Michio Ito, and sent them to a relocation center. "With a

Three U.S. battleships are hit during the Japanese attack on Pearl Harbor on December 7, 1941. Japan's bombing of U.S. military bases at Pearl Harbor brought the United States into World War II.

flash I realized that I was no longer the sculptor alone," Noguchi later recalled in his autobiography. "I was not just American but Nisei."

Noguchi's father, Yonejiro, had been vocally anti-American for several years. He had made statements supporting Japan's plan to free Asia from what he considered Western (or American) imperialism. Several years before Pearl Harbor, the Japanese consulate in New York had asked Noguchi to make a pro-Japanese statement like his father's, the "patriotic poet." Ironically, shortly afterward, the American State Department asked Noguchi to send an open letter to his father condemning his sentiments. Noguchi refused both requests. He didn't want to publicly attack his father, and he didn't want to come down squarely on the side of either country. Now, though, during the period of paranoia following Pearl Harbor, he was, without question, a nisei.

Between the Generations: JAPANESE IMMIGRATION TO THE UNITED STATES

From 1861 to 1940, about 275,000 Japanese people moved to Hawaii and to the American mainland. A few events set this emigration in motion. The first was the opening of Japan's ports of trade in 1854, after 200 years of isolation. The flood of American products into their country prompted a fascination with the advanced Western world and started a dialogue between the two nations. In 1882, Congress passed the Chinese Exclusion Act, barring any further Chinese immigration. This opened up a lot of agricultural jobs up and down the West Coast.

Before 1907, the Japanese immigrants were mostly men, and they came to America to work the farms. After 1907, thousands of Japanese women made the journey to join their husbands or to marry. Life was hard for these families. In addition to having to adjust to a new country with its foreign customs and culture, the immigrants were given the least desirable land to farm. Plus, the prejudice they suffered is evidenced by the laws passed by Congress during these years—in 1900, issei (Japanese immigrants) were barred from attaining citizenship. In addition, in California and other western states, they were also barred from owning land, which significantly handicapped their chances for success. Despite these obstacles, many did well—which only increased the hostility of their white neighbors.

Within this context, Yone Noguchi's experience was unusual. He walked off the steamship *Belgic* in 1893 and went directly to

In February 1942, President Roosevelt signed Executive Order 9066, authorizing military authorities to evacuate all Japanese aliens and all American-born people of Japanese descent from the West Coast. The issei and nisei had 10 days to close up their businesses and homes. More than 100,000 people were loaded on trains and buses and sent to assembly centers

San Francisco, where there were thousands of Chinese immigrants but only 1,000 or so Japanese. He wrote that most of the Japanese he saw living in San Francisco's Japantown were laborers who "lived like dogs and pigs." He had no interest in working in the fields or the fish market, so he made his own way, eventually landing in a classroom at Stanford University, which, luckily, did not charge tuition. His poetry was warmly received because of the interest at that time in "Oriental" culture.

When Isamu Noguchi moved back to America as a teenager in 1918, he ended up in rural Indiana, in a place where he was the only Japanese person for many miles around. He was called "the boy from Asia," "Oriental," or a "Jap." Not all of America was the same, however. Leaving the Midwest for New York City in 1923 was like entering a new country. There, Isamu met many Japanese Americans, well-educated and successful in everything from science to the arts. Cosmopolitan New York was largely a refuge from the waves of prejudice that swelled in the United States during the years before and during World War II. If Yone had remained in the United States, he would have suffered more hardships than his son during these years of great prejudice against the Japanese. As an issei, Yone would have been considered an "enemy alien" and may have been placed in a detention camp.

and then on to larger camps that were constructed in "safe" rural areas of Arkansas, Arizona, Idaho, Utah, Colorado, and Wyoming. All they were allowed to carry with them was hand luggage. Estimates of the value of property confiscated from Japanese Americans ran as high as $400 million. The extent of personal trauma that they suffered is impossible to measure, or even to imagine.

For Noguchi, the turmoil pushed art into the background. He decided he "wanted to do something as an American" for the war effort, so he organized Nisei Writers and Artists for Democracy, in San Francisco. Isamu's "celebrity" status attracted attention for the group, whose mission was to prevent compulsory relocation by explaining to the authorities and the public that being an American citizen was about much more than ancestry and blood.

Noguchi hoped to testify at the congressional hearings being held in San Francisco to evaluate the need for evacuations. He said a few words, but he was disappointed that he was overshadowed by celebrities like Joe DiMaggio's mother speaking on behalf of Italian-American and German refugees, who solicited sympathy with their stories of fleeing from the Nazis.

To record this bizarre moment in time, he and his friends made a documentary about the relocation. Its goal was ambiguous. Noguchi wrote in a memo about the making of the film that it could function as any of the following: "propaganda, a legal document, a sociological study, a demonstration of democracy under trying circumstances, or a moving human story." By the time it was ready to screen, the evacuation protocol had expanded to include anyone with a drop of Japanese blood. Visitors were allowed to return home, so Noguchi left California for New York. There he tried to drum up concern for what was happening on the opposite coast, but only a few offered to help him spread the word.

During a trip to Washington, D.C., John Collier, the commissioner of Indian Affairs, asked Noguchi to help set up one

Noguchi tried to make life better for the evacuees at the War Relocation Authority center in Poston, Arizona. This photograph shows the camp's living quarters.

of the internment camps in Poston, Arizona. He was meant to promote arts and crafts among the evacuees and teach them skills that would ease their transition back into society following their internment. Noguchi enthusiastically agreed to "self-incarcerate" himself in Arizona in order to help create a model community. When he returned to New York, he called on eight other prominent Japanese-American artists to join him in volunteering to work at relocation camps. No one stepped up. One even told Noguchi that his idea was crazy.

Less than a month after he returned to New York, in May 1942, Noguchi flew to Los Angeles to retrieve his car. He then drove to the Poston relocation camp, located in the middle of the Arizona desert. The baking heat of the sun and the treeless wide-open landscape must have been reminiscent of his first impression of Rolling Prairie, Indiana. The camp itself was under construction. When it was finished, there were 800 low, wooden barracks and communal mess halls and washrooms. The whole camp was surrounded by barbed wire and watchtowers armed by men with machine guns. The internees had been evacuated under the pretense of their own protection, but the camp certainly looked more like a prison than a refuge.

The internees began pouring in soon after Noguchi arrived. There were 17,000 people in all, each with his or her own serial number. A siren woke them at 7:00 A.M. Their daily life consisted mostly of waiting in lines—for the bathroom, the shower, the food, the toilet. In a letter to a fellow artist, Noguchi wrote, "This is the weirdest, most unreal situation—like in a dream—I wish I were out. . . . Our sphere of effective activity is cut to a minimum. Our preoccupations are the intense dry heat, the afternoon dust storms, the food." He actively tried to improve his and the internees' situation by drawing up plans for baseball fields, parks, swimming pools, an irrigation system. He opened up a woodcarving and carpentry shop. But the War Relocation Authority (WRA) officials turned down his plans and refused to get him supplies or tools for the woodworking shop.

Noguchi was despondent over his ineffectiveness—and the WRA's lackluster response to his efforts. Later, he wrote, "It soon became apparent that the purpose of the War Relocation Authority was hopelessly at odds with that ideal cooperative community pictured by Mr. Collier. They wanted nothing permanent, nor pleasant." Perhaps the WRA resisted building anything permanent because they didn't want to create mementos of the time America imprisoned an entire segment of its own population.

He also was finding it difficult to connect with the other niseis, who were suspicious of him because of his seemingly

Isamu Noguchi works on a sculpture in his studio in New York City in September 1946.

special position. He had a big room all to himself, whereas the others were crammed into small spaces. They wondered if he was an agent for the people who rounded them up and herded them to the desert. Also, they were mostly younger—their average age was 18—and they were mostly farmers with little education. At the same time, he wasn't about to befriend the American administrators, who wouldn't even deign to take his initiatives seriously. He felt more isolated than ever. In a letter to Collier, he wrote: "I am extremely despondent for lack of companionship." Soon, he couldn't wait to leave Poston, but his volunteer status seemed to have changed overnight to prisoner, as he needed permission to leave. The WRA had to authorize his release. He was there for six and a half months—almost four of those months were spent waiting for his release.

After he returned to New York, he never spoke of his difficulties at the camp. He was relieved to be free. In his autobiography he wrote, "The deep depression that comes with living under a cloud of suspicion, which we Nisei experienced, lifted, and was followed by tranquility. I was free finally of all causes. . . . I resolved henceforth to be an artist only."

9

Healing His Wounds

Back in New York, Isamu Noguchi rented a studio on Mac-Dougal Street in Greenwich Village. He worked during the day in his studio and attended artists' gatherings in the evening. He tried to shake off the negative experience of the internment camp. The concentration and labor that went into creating stone sculpture was for him "a ceremony of exorcism to wipe away the distress that had built in my soul." In the 1940s, New York was filled with emerging American artists. There, they mingled with the European artists who had fled their war-torn homelands. New styles were crystallizing, including abstract expressionism and surrealism. The city was full of energy. In 1942, Peggy Guggenheim, who launched the careers of many famous modern artists, opened her Art of This Century Gallery, and it became a regular gathering place for artists in the scene.

Isamu dabbled in these new styles and tried sculpting with all kinds of materials, including string, driftwood, bones, paper, wire, wood, and magnesite. He also turned to industrial design, designing a coffee table for the Herman Miller Furniture Company that sold so well, it is still manufactured today.

Noguchi was also commissioned to design a stage set for a dance production by Martha Graham, whose portrait bust he'd sculpted in 1928. He'd met Graham through his sister, Ailes, who danced in her company. Isamu would end up collaborating with Graham on 22 more stage sets. He enjoyed the challenge of designing a dynamic environment that enhanced the drama being played out onstage and that made the audience feel connected to the dancers. Noguchi also made the first incarnation of his *akari* ("light") lamps. Noguchi said his dismal experience at the internment camp inspired him to turn light into art. *Lunar Infant* was a light sculpture made from rough hemp cloth reinforced with magnesite and lit from within by the soft glow of an electric bulb. The name evoked the refuge that is a mother's womb. The piece may have been unconsciously influenced by Isamu's experience as a toddler in Tokyo, watching sunlight filter through the shoji screens in his and Leonie's first Japanese home.

During this fruitful time of experimentation, Noguchi was completely taken aback by the arrival at his door of a deportation order. Apparently, the FBI had categorized him as a possible threat, because he was the son of a Japanese nationalist. It hadn't helped that he'd written an article for the *New Republic* magazine that made known his sympathies with the internees in the camps. Furthermore, when he'd been handed a loyalty pledge to sign when he left Poston, he'd refused to pledge his loyalty to the United States. The American Civil Liberties Union defended Isamu's right to remain an American citizen, and eventually the deportation order was dropped. Noguchi, though, was very deeply wounded by the attempt of authorities to send him back to Japan. After all, he had been born an American, and he had tried to do something in the war effort out of a sincere sense of duty as an American.

Isamu Noguchi displays his *Light Sculpture* in 1944.

In May 1945, Germany surrendered to the Allied troops in Europe, but war raged on in the Pacific. To bring the conflict to a speedier end, the U.S. military bombed the Japanese city of Hiroshima on August 6, obliterating the city. When Japan didn't surrender, another bomb was dropped two days later on Nagasaki. On August 9, Japan surrendered, and World War II finally came to an end.

In 1946, Noguchi was included in an art show called "Fourteen Americans," at the Museum of Modern Art. It was considered the first important postwar exhibition of new trends in American art. Along with Noguchi, the exhibit included such artists as Robert Motherwell, Arshile Gorky, and David Hare. Noguchi spent the winter of 1945–1946 creating *Kouros* by cutting and polishing marble slabs and fitting them together using interlocking slots, almost like fitting logs together to make a log cabin. In this case, form had followed function—flat marble slabs were much more affordable at that time in New York than large blocks of marble. *Kouros*, more than 9 feet (2.8 meters) tall, was made from pink marble rippled with gray.

Art Digest said that Noguchi was "achieving the intangible . . . through the abstract." The prestigious Metropolitan Museum of Art bought *Kouros* for its permanent collection. *Art News* featured an eight-page spread on Noguchi, naming him "one of America's most distinguished yet least-known artists." He had come into his own.

Still, critics didn't know what to make of Noguchi. He worked in so many styles, he was impossible to pigeonhole. As soon as he began to create a body of work in one style, he was off exploring another. In 1949, he was literally off and exploring again, thanks to a Bollingen Foundation grant. The income allowed Noguchi to travel the world to research a book about sculpture as it relates to "leisure." He'd reached what he considered a dead-end artistically—he'd mastered what he set out to master, and he was in search of new inspiration. He intended to wander the world to study the work of ancient sculptors by touring the remains of monuments and sacred sites imbued with public meaning.

First, Noguchi went to India, by way of Paris, Italy, Greece, and Egypt. He carried his Leica camera with him everywhere.

Isamu Noguchi's 1943 *Monument to Heroes* is a painted cardboard, wood, bone and string sculpture that expresses his revulsion of war.

Those who accompanied him remember him snapping pictures of everything, "like a man possessed." He toured India for seven months and was most impressed by the eighteenth-century observatories composed of great stone sundials, pits dug into the earth, and stairwells that ended abruptly as they climbed toward the sky. He noted that sculpture in India was assigned religious meaning and often played a part in ceremonies. In an interview, he noted, "[O]ur aesthetic appreciation of this sculpture is quite different from our appreciation of the sculptures we see on pedestals in our art museums." For example, he saw many *lingam*, stone objects related to the god Shiva that worshippers used while praying for the prosperity of their descendants. In contrast, in museums people are removed from the art, almost as if there's an invisible wall between the person and the sculpture.

On May 2, 1950, at the age of 46, Isamu Noguchi arrived in Japan for the third time in his life. He'd lost touch with his father and half-siblings during the war. For a long time, he didn't know whether they were alive or dead. Some may have fought in the army. Others may have perished in the bombings. At the end of the war, American bombs had reduced much of Tokyo to rubble. In 1947, however, while Isamu was being interviewed for a Japanese newspaper, he asked the reporter to find out whether Yonejiro was alive. It turns out that he was fine. He and his family had been evacuated during the war, and they were living outside Tokyo.

Yonejiro wrote a letter to Isamu, and it is obvious from his tone that Yonejiro had mellowed in his old age. He wrote, "I know you are doing a very distinguished work of which I feel so applaud [sic]. Oh if your mother is living today and sees of you today!" He also mentioned in his letter that he and his family had lost much in the war and that they were in dire financial straits. Isamu was overjoyed to hear from his father, and he immediately sent packages with clothes, shoes, and other necessities.

Yonejiro died from stomach cancer in July of that year. Before he passed on, however, he made it known to Isamu how proud he was of his accomplishments. "Your letter of May 15 reached me safely," he wrote, "and it made me cry from joy and I could not speak for some moment." One of Isamu's half-brothers reported to him that Yonejiro had cried when he heard how famous his son had become and that he'd hoped that they would see each other again.

That feeling seemed to have spread among all of Noguchi's relatives in Japan. He was met at the airport by three half-brothers and by Yonejiro's widow, the very one who had objected to her husband meeting with his illegitimate son when Isamu was last in Japan, in 1917. Now, everything was forgiven.

All the major newspapers carried a photo of Isamu arriving in Tokyo. When the reporters asked why he came to Japan he said, "I want to meet young Japanese artists and architects. There is a new world emerging in Asia, and I think it is extremely important to learn what the new generation here is doing and also trying to do." Noguchi was a respected global artist and he hailed from New York, the nexus of the modern art world. His advice was in demand. A line formed three hours before he was scheduled to give a public lecture on art and his year-long journey. His main advice for young artists in postwar Japan was to resist being too influenced by Western culture. Instead, he told them, look to your own heritage for inspiration. "To be authentic," he told them, "is to be modern." Headlines the day after his lecture read "America Envies Japan's Beauty" and "Don't Lose Individuality."

In Tokyo, Noguchi was wined and dined, but as usual, he was restless and anxious to tour the country with his Leica. He spent two weeks in Kyoto visiting temples and gardens in the ancient city, and he paid special attention to the Japanese gardens. Noguchi made a trip to Chigasaki to see the Triangle House, and he visited Keio University, where his father had taught literature for 40 years. He was asked to design a faculty room for a building on campus and he immediately agreed. He saw it as further validation from the Japanese people that they thought of him as

THE ART OF JAPANESE GARDENS

What makes a Japanese garden different from a French or English garden? The key lies in the difference in how each culture sees nature. In the West, throughout time, nature and man have been engaged in an epic struggle. This perspective manifests itself in gardens of the West—English, French, Italian—where nature is tamed and held at bay by man-made designs and structures. In an English garden, for example, you're likely to find a hedge trimmed into a large boxy shape, a lawn clipped short, and a bed of roses laid out in tidy rows.

In the East, in Asian cultures, people have historically perceived nature as a peer and an ally—in ancient Japan, people believed that God's spirit resided in nature. They thought that this spirit was especially strong in stones and in ponds. Nature was seen as an entity to be celebrated and revered. The gardens that Isamu Noguchi saw in and near Kyoto were *shuyu* ("stroll") style. They have paths that meander through the landscape so that a different view unfurls in front of the visitor as he makes his way from one point to the next. Designers order the placement of each stone, tree, and pond in a shuyu garden to carefully manage the visitor's experience.

Zen gardens, also called dry-mountain-water gardens, do not use water, and they make much use of symbolism. Groups of rocks represent mountains or waterfalls, and white sand symbolizes flowing water. They're meant to be gazed on from a nearby vantage point, not entered physically. Tea gardens, on the other hand, are meant to be used rather than contemplated. They function as a transition from the day-to-day world to the quiet, understated interior of the tea house—their stepping stones and stone lanterns show visitors the way. Still another type of Japanese garden, the pond or landscape garden, incorporates scenes in miniature, such as scenes from history or poetry. Of course, not all gardens are completely Eastern or Western in style—hybrids have cropped up as the different cultures have influenced one another.

one of their own. He created a room that blended Eastern and Western functions. In Japanese culture, it's normal to sit cross-legged on the floor instead of sitting on a chair. He designed the room at three different elevations, so people could sit on the floor, stand, or sit on chairs, and still coexist on the same level.

People in Japan were so anxious to see his work that he planned a solo exhibition and worked feverishly to create sculptures for the show. Noguchi made fast friends with several fellow Japanese artists about his age, and before he left, they threw him a festive good-bye party. Finally Noguchi had found a group of people who valued him for who he was. He boarded a plane to the United States (a much faster way to travel than the boats he had taken the last two times he came to Japan) with the intention of returning to Japan as soon as possible. Basically, he was only going to make enough money to return to what he called "the New Japan."

In New York, he spent his time arranging exhibits for his Japanese friends and looking for materials to send to the Japan Craft Center in Tokyo. He also met a Japanese film star named Yoshiko Yamaguchi. They married in 1951. All the Japanese newspapers carried the story of this celebrity wedding. The newlyweds surprised the press by moving into a farmhouse on the property of Rosanjin Kitaoji, a potter, who lived in Kamakura, an old city an hour south of Tokyo. In Rosanjin, Noguchi found another mentor and a new kind of lifestyle.

On his first visit to Rosanjin's estate, Noguchi was amazed and impressed by the beautiful six acres of hills and fields that lay at the end of a narrow country road. Rosanjin had built his own kiln, so he was able to live and work on this private compound. To Noguchi, this ideal setting was like a dream. After he complimented the place, Rosanjin invited him and his wife to stay there.

Their house there was one-story, and it was long and narrow like one of the "eel's-bed" townhouses in Kyoto. It consisted of three rooms laid out in a straight line. It was a traditional-style

Isamu Noguchi's 1943-44 *Red Lunar Fist* is a magnesite, cement, plastic, resin, and electric light sculpture.

Japanese house with no modern amenities—there was no in-door plumbing. Isamu and Yoshiko used an outdoor privy. He fired his clay in Rosanjin's kiln and loved working with the un-predictable material. "In ceramic art there are elements beyond our control," he wrote in an essay in 1952. "One can say that it is both easy and difficult. It is also both fragile and enduring. Like ink painting, it does not permit change or hesitation. The best ceramic work is not carefully designed. It lets nature speak through it." The secluded life he led there was acceptable to Isamu, but not to Yoshiko. She had always lived in Western-style houses and had never had to use an outhouse. She was usually away, however, filming movies on location.

After five months at Rosanjin's estate, Noguchi exhibited his pottery at a show in Kamakura. He used clay to create modern sculptural forms. Clay, normally a utilitarian material, was used in this context to express his vision. No one had really seen the material used before in this manner. Noguchi also exhibited his akari lamps, made from Japanese paper and bamboo. The lamps were modern in design but crafted from traditional Japanese

In 1953, Noguchi's wife, actress Yoshiko "Shirley" Yamaguchi was interviewed by reporters after the American embassy announced that the U. S. State Department was refusing the young actress a visa for entry into the United States. No explanation was given.

materials. For Noguchi, they represented a modern interpretation of an old tradition. The Japanese critics weren't ready for this—they all but ignored the akari lamps in their reviews. The akari lamps even puzzled the sponsors of the exhibition, who didn't consider them a form of sculpture.

Noguchi's honeymoon with Japan came to an end when he was asked to build a monument to peace in Hiroshima, where America and its allies dropped the atomic bomb in 1945. The city and its inhabitants were devastated by the bomb, and Noguchi considered it a great honor to be asked to work on the memorial. He worked extremely hard coming up with a design for an "Arch of Peace." It was a black granite arch of which only the top third was visible. The rest was underground, where the cylinders framed a chamber that held a granite box cantilevered from the wall and engraved with the names of the bomb victims. Ultimately, his design was rejected because he was deemed a foreigner. Noguchi was extremely disappointed. In his museum catalog, he writes, "Was it because I was an American, or was it a case of someone not having the proper authorization to which my proposal fell victim?" He predicted that the arch "would've become a representative monument of the twentieth century." He felt that the hopes he'd placed on postwar Japan had been an illusion.

10

Citizen of
the World

For the rest of the 1950s, Noguchi flew back and forth from New York to Japan to Paris, working alongside architects on large-scale gardens and designing public space. For these projects, he often searched for stones in Japanese quarries. He called it "fishing" for stones. Garden design in the West, however, was seen as a less serious art form than sculpture or painting. Consequently, Noguchi was criticized for straying from his role as a "true artist." In the East, though, as Gordon Bunshaft, one of his architect collaborators, pointed out, there was no separation to the arts: A pot was considered as important as a painting. Certainly Noguchi put as much thought into his gardens as he did into his sculptures. He said, "In all my gardens there is something a little off-balance somewhere. But isn't that like life? There's no such thing as a perfect life." Just like life, it seemed there was no such thing as a perfect marriage—he and Yamaguchi divorced in 1956.

"For me," Noguchi later recalled in John Gordon's biography of the artist, "the 1960s was a 'great beginning.' " He finally put down roots—in both the United States and Japan. He bought a small factory building in Long Island City, across the East River from Manhattan, and carved out a small area for his living quarters. The rest of the building was a workspace outfitted with a chain-hoist for moving large stones. In Japan, he set up a workshop in Mure, near the quarries where he went to "fish" for stones. Just as easily as he had accumulated mentors throughout his career, now he attracted apprentices and protégés. Young sculptors would show up at his door, hoping to learn at the feet of the master. In Mure, he was lucky to have help from Masatoshi Izumi, the third-oldest son of a family that had been stonecutters for several generations. Isamu was nearly 60 when he met 25-year-old Izumi. He was dubious of the young man's skill, so he tested him. He took three small plaster models from his pocket and asked him to reproduce them in stone. When he returned, Izumi had done so, perfectly.

Noguchi insisted on cutting and polishing everything by hand. He refused to use machines for sanding or cutting—and this was challenging, as he worked on enormous blocks of stone. His sculpture *Black Sun* began as a 35-ton chunk of black Brazilian granite that stood 10 feet (3 meters) high. He delighted in the process. He wrote, "There is a sequence to stone working. First, the rear half is removed with drill holes and wedges. Afterward comes the carving, splitting with the 'genno,' the sledgehammer used for knocking off large hunks."

At Mure, he duplicated the hermit-like, work-intense, self-contained universe that he had witnessed in Brancusi's studio in Paris and at Rosanjin's estate in Kamakura in the 1950s. The 200-year-old home faced distant mountains, as his childhood home had in Chigasaki. The interior was simple, with tatami mats and shoji screens, and very little of the odds and ends of everyday life. Electronics, such as his record player and TV set, were concealed behind wooden panels.

On display in the middle of the front room was a sculpture called *Wave in Space*. This work was much different from the

A pair of huge stones sits outside the Isamu Noguchi Garden Museum in the southern Japanese village of Mure. Called the *Circle*, the dirt yard in the village served as one of Noguchi's main workshops from the late 1960s.

wave he created in kindergarten. The wave was carved from a block of black granite, and the sculpture stood as high as a low table. It almost looked like it was meant to be a table, except for the rounded form that swelled up in the middle. Noguchi seemed to delight in challenging people's perceptions of seemingly well-understood concepts such as waves and gravity. His sculpture *Red Cube*, a massive cube made of steel, balances delicately on one point in the plaza in front of Marine Midland Bank in the financial district of Manhattan. The enormous cube seems weightless. Noguchi said in his autobiography that *Red Cube* signified chance, "like the rolling of the dice"—something that people who work on Wall Street do every day.

Outside his house in Mure, Noguchi created a large work-circle, where he carved and cut his stone. At this point, he was working mostly with hard granites and basalts that are found in Japan. Sometimes he'd spend years on a single piece, considering it from afar until he decided—or until it decided for him—exactly what shape it should take. "These are private sculptures," he later wrote in *The Isamu Noguchi Garden Museum*, "a dialogue between myself and the primary matter of the universe. A meditation, if you will, that carries me on and on one step after another." It took nine years (1957–1966) for Noguchi to consider *Myo* finished. At one point, Masatoshi Izumi described picking Noguchi up from the airport and arriving at Mure, just to watch the artist run inside the house and throw on his work clothes, anxious to act on an epiphany he had while he was away about where to cut one of the boulders in his circle.

Noguchi began to think about his legacy. What would people think of him and his work when he passed on? What was he leaving to the world? A good friend and patron urged him to write an autobiography. *A Sculptor's World* was published in 1968. In it, Noguchi emphasized his unique position as an artist straddling two cultures. The same year, the Whitney Museum in New York held a retrospective of his work. Once again, critics found him difficult to categorize because his work was so new in and of itself—and at the same time, it borrowed from so many artistic eras and styles.

Noguchi only continued to reinvent himself. In 1970, he was commissioned to design a fountain for the Osaka World's Fair. As he wrote in his museum catalog, "I approached the work as something of a challenge to the commonly held idea of fountains as water spurting upward. My fountains jetted down one hundred feet, rotated, sprayed, and swirled water, disappeared and reappeared as mist." He designed two fountains—one looks like a giant, boxy cheese grater suspended high in the air. The other resembles two donut-shaped coins that intersect. Water is released from both forms in varying degrees of water pressure.

MASTER OF MANY MATERIALS

Isamu Noguchi was best known for carving stone, but he actually worked with many types of material and in many forms, from sculpture to furniture to theater sets. In addition to the following, Noguchi worked with water, light, wood, magnesite, sound, and stone.

Clay: Noguchi created all his clay pieces while he was living in or visiting Japan, first in 1931 in Kyoto and again during his third visit to Japan, beginning in 1950. On this third visit, he lived on a house on the estate of Rosanjin Kitaoji, a famous ceramist whose kiln and studio were on his property. This is what Noguchi said about working with clay: "The attractions of ceramics lie partly in its contradictions. It is both difficult and easy, with an element beyond our control. It is both extremely fragile and durable. . . . It does not lend itself to erasures and indecision. . . . I associate it with the closeness of earth and wood which is for me Japan and not America today."

Metal: The artist started working in metal while he was in Paris in the late 1920s, apprenticing with Constantin Brancusi. He made works out of bent sheets of polished brass. He also worked later with other types of metal, including sheet metal and galvanized steel. Here is what Noguchi said about what inspired him to work with metal: "It seemed absurd to me to be working with rocks and stones in New York, where walls of glass and steel are our horizon, and our landscape is that of boxes piled high in the air."

Paper: Some people only know Noguchi as the artist who designed the Noguchi lamp. They're talking about akari lamps, made from bamboo and paper. Noguchi's inspiration in creating akari lamps was Japanese shoji screens. Noguchi had this to say about his akari lamps: "Looking more fragile than they are, akari seem to float, casting their light as in passing. They do not encumber our space as mass or as a possession; if they hardly exist in use, when not in use they fold away in an envelope. They perch light as a feather, some pinned to the wall, others clipped to a cord, and all may be moved with the thought."

People marveled at the spectacle and remarked upon the patterns of mist, the sound of water rushing from the jets, and the reflections produced by the interaction of the water.

The projects he worked on from 1970 until his death in 1988 continued to fuse all his experiences and the intense studies he made during his travels. For example, in a public sculpture in Cleveland, he used a utilitarian material—sewer pipe—to create a form that is sculpturally linked to the cylindrical form of haniwa.

Noguchi remained disappointed that he never had a chance to complete his Hiroshima memorial, but he did come on a meaningful commission late in life. A California business owner came to his home in Long Island City in 1979 to ask him to design something for a site near San Diego, in California. The man had been raised on the land, which was once the largest lima bean farm in the United States. He had bought and developed the former farmland. He turned it into the site of South Coast Plaza, the largest shopping mall in California. He commissioned sculptures to beautify its outdoor spaces, but he wanted Noguchi specifically to figure out what to do with a large plot of land sandwiched between two buildings. Noguchi created *California Scenario* as an ode to those drawn to California, as his mother had been, by its promise.

Noguchi opened the Noguchi Museum in a building next to his office and studio in Long Island City in 1985. In the museum catalog, he wrote, "This museum and catalogue attempt to define my role as a crossing where inward and outward meet, East and West." He saved most of his favorite works over the years, selling pieces only when he needed money to fund his travels. The museum director was surprised at how meticulously he'd kept all of his receipts, work orders, correspondence, and press from over the years. It was almost as if he was planning from a very young age to be famous. In his last years, he received several major awards, including the National Medal of the Arts, presented to him by President Ronald Reagan. It was a great

Noguchi sits on a curved wall inside the Noguchi-Rose Sculpture Garden at the Israel Museum in Jerusalem, Israel, in May 1965.

honor to be asked to design the entirety of the American pavilion at the 1986 Venice Biennale.

Still, Noguchi never felt as though he was understood completely. He wrote a few months before his death that he was an expatriate wherever he went. Late in life he told an interviewer, "I was born bearing the burden of two countries, and I have never ceased searching to answer where is my native place, where I can find a peaceful life, where is there a place where I can be of use." On December 30, 1988, Noguchi died of pneumonia. True to form, his ashes were scattered around the world—at the Isamu Noguchi Garden Museum, in Long Island City; at Mure; and off the coast of Maui, in the ocean that links his motherland to his fatherland.

Since his death, Noguchi has continued to gain the respect of the public. In the twenty-first century, a whole century after his birth, his furniture and lamp designs are more popular than ever. In the 1990s, mid-century furniture and industrial design enjoyed a healthy resurgence, and Noguchi is one of the designers whose work rode this wave. Designs including his free-form couches and ottomans, coffee table, and akari lamps went back into production. Finally, if the true sign of success is being copied, well, then, Noguchi is enormously successful. People may have been puzzled by his paper and bamboo lamps when he first displayed them, but today imitations abound.

Noguchi joked in his autobiography that someone had once told him they saw a sign in a shop window for "Noguchi-type lamps," so he confronted the shop owner. The fellow said, "If you don't like it, why don't you design me one?" Noguchi writes, "When I devised what I thought was a contribution, all he could say was, 'Sorry, that's not a Noguchi-style lamp.' " One wonders what Isamu would think of the Noguchi-style lamps being peddled at IKEA today.

Meanwhile, Noguchi's originals continue to set records at auction houses. In December 2005, one of his coffee tables sold for $630,000 at an auction in Chicago—and that was about $530,000 more than the auction house had predicted. In 1949, when it was made, this record-setting table could have been bought for less than $300. A month earlier, a magnesite maquette (or model) that Noguchi made for a playground design

Noguchi's eight-ton, 11½ foot tall sculpture *Unidentified Object* stands at the entrance to Central Park in New York City.

fetched $216,000 at an auction in New Jersey. The auction house, however, thought it would go for about $185,000 less. When will people stop underestimating Isamu Noguchi?

Art historians agree that that Noguchi was misunderstood and undervalued. Unlike Jackson Pollock or Mark Rothko, whose names are almost synonymous with abstract expressionism, or Salvador Dali, who immediately brings to mind surrealism, Noguchi didn't embody a single style. As one critic wrote, "It is as if there are too many Noguchis to hold in the mind." Art historian Dore Ashton wrote, "Such misunderstanding . . . reflects only on the very culture that Noguchi sought to surpass, the cliché-ridden, nationalistic, materialistic culture that he wished to supersede with a new conception of sculptured space." Noguchi didn't embody a single style; he was truly a citizen of the world. Since his death, people have begun to understand him more in hindsight. Our growing understanding of Noguchi might have made sense to Noguchi himself, who told an interviewer shortly before his death, "Real sculpture is what you don't immediately see. Sculpture is what you find."

CHRONOLOGY

1904 *November 17* Isamu Noguchi is born in Los Angeles to American writer/editor Leonie Gilmour and Japanese poet Yonejiro Noguchi.

1907 Young Isamu moves to Japan with Leonie. He lives in Tokyo, Chigasaki, and Yokohama, and attends Japanese and Jesuit schools.

1912 His sister, Ailes, is born.

1918 Leonie sends Isamu to Interlaken School, near Rolling Prairie, Indiana; he later lived with the Mack family in LaPorte.

1922 Isamu graduates from high school in LaPorte as Isamu Gilmour. He spends the summer in Stamford, Connecticut, as apprentice to Gutzon Borglum. Isamu moves to New York and enrolls at Columbia University as a premedical student.

1923 Leonie returns to California after 17 years in Japan.

1924 Encouraged by director Onorio Ruotolo, he decides to become a sculptor.

1924 Noguchi sets up his first studio.

1927–1928 Noguchi receives a Guggenheim Fellowship. He goes to Paris and serves as Constantin Brancusi's studio assistant for seven months.

1929 He exhibits abstractions in his first one-man show at Eugene Schoen Gallery in April.

1930 Noguchi does his first portrait exhibition. He studies brush drawing with Ch'i Pai-shih in Peking.

1931 He spends seven months in Japan. He works in clay with potter Uno Jinmatsu.

1932 Noguchi has three shows in New York.

1933–1934 Noguchi works briefly for Public Works of Art Project. He spends the summer of 1934 in Woodstock, New York, sculpting *Death*.

1935 He exhibits *Death* and designs his first theater set for Martha Graham's *Frontier*.

1936 Noguchi spends eight months in Mexico City.

1938–1939 Noguchi wins a competition to create the Associated Press Building plaque, *News*.

1942 Noguchi volunteers to spend six months in a Japanese-American relocation camp in Arizona.

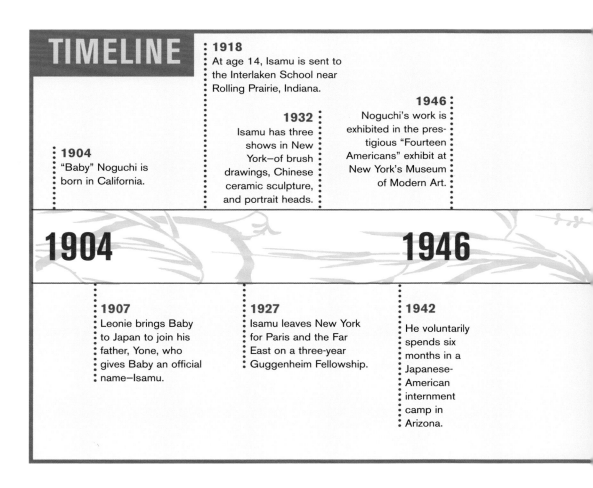

TIMELINE

1918
At age 14, Isamu is sent to the Interlaken School near Rolling Prairie, Indiana.

1932
Isamu has three shows in New York—of brush drawings, Chinese ceramic sculpture, and portrait heads.

1946
Noguchi's work is exhibited in the prestigious "Fourteen Americans" exhibit at New York's Museum of Modern Art.

1904
"Baby" Noguchi is born in California.

1904

1946

1907
Leonie brings Baby to Japan to join his father, Yone, who gives Baby an official name—Isamu.

1927
Isamu leaves New York for Paris and the Far East on a three-year Guggenheim Fellowship.

1942
He voluntarily spends six months in a Japanese-American internment camp in Arizona.

1943 Noguchi makes his first lunar-illuminated sculptures (predecessors of akari lamps).

1946 Works by Noguchi are exhibited in "Fourteen Americans" at the Museum of Modern Art, New York.

1949 Noguchi does his first one-man exhibition in New York since 1935 at the Egan Gallery.

1950–1952 He arrives in Japan and begins designing akari lamps. He works extensively with clay, and meets and marries actress Yoshiko Yamaguchi.

1956–1958 Noguchi does a garden for the UNESCO building in Paris.

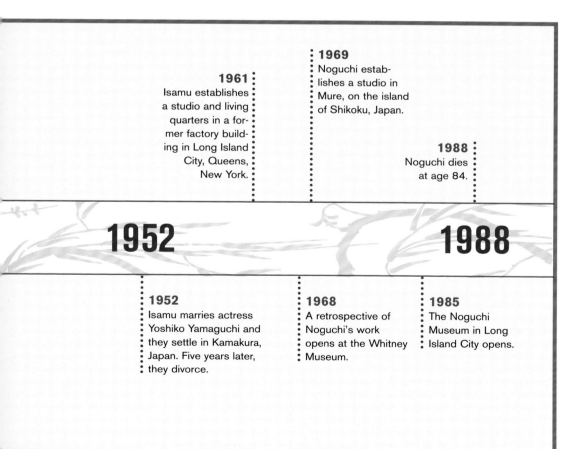

1961
Isamu establishes a studio and living quarters in a former factory building in Long Island City, Queens, New York.

1969
Noguchi establishes a studio in Mure, on the island of Shikoku, Japan.

1988
Noguchi dies at age 84.

1952

1988

1952
Isamu marries actress Yoshiko Yamaguchi and they settle in Kamakura, Japan. Five years later, they divorce.

1968
A retrospective of Noguchi's work opens at the Whitney Museum.

1985
The Noguchi Museum in Long Island City opens.

1961 Noguchi exhibits metal and balsawood pieces at Cordier & Warren Gallery. He does his first plaza, for First National City Bank, in Fort Worth, Texas. He establishes his studio at 33-38 Tenth Street, Long Island City, New York.

1962–1966 He does gardens for Chase Manhattan Bank, IBM, Beinecke Library at Yale, and the Israel Museum in Jerusalem.

1968 A retrospective of Noguchi's work is held at the Whitney Museum. He publishes his autobiography, *A Sculptor's World*.

1969 Noguchi establishes a studio in Mure, on the island of Shikoku, Japan.

1972–1973 Noguchi holds exhibitions in galleries in New York, London, Zurich, and Tokyo.

1974–1978 He acquires the 33-37 Vernon Boulevard building in Long Island City in order to open a museum.

1979–1981 A documentary film on Noguchi's work and life is made and shown on PBS. He establishes the Noguchi Foundation.

1982–1983 Noguchi creates the *California Scenario* garden in Costa Mesa, California, and a plaza and sculpture for the Japanese-American Cultural and Community Center in Los Angeles.

1984 Noguchi receives an Israel Museum Fellowship in Jerusalem and the President's Medal of Honor.

1985 Isamu Noguchi Garden Museum in Long Island City opens to the public.

1987 His catalogue for the Isamu Noguchi Museum is published, and he receives the National Medal of Arts, presented by President Ronald Reagan.

1988 Isamu Noguchi dies, after a short illness, on December 30, at age 84.

GLOSSARY

akari—Translates to "light." Noguchi used the word *akari* to refer to the lamps he designed that are made from bamboo strips and mulberry bark paper.

baka gaijin—Translates to "dumb foreigner."

haniwa—From the third to sixth centuries in Japan, enormous tombs were built for aristocrats and military leaders. Haniwa figurines were positioned around and in front of these tombs to act as attendants to the departed, guardians of the tomb, and symbols to all who passed by of the elite status of the tomb's inhabitant. Though the direct translation is "clay rings," haniwa took many forms, including horses, chickens, birds, houses, swords, shields, and humans.

issei—Translates to "first-generation"; this term was used to describe Japanese Americans who were born in Japan and emigrated to America before World War II. Between 1860 and 1940, about 275,000 Japanese people moved to Hawaii and the continental United States. They were declared "enemy aliens" once the United States declared war on Japan on December 8, 1941.

Japonisme—When Japanese ports reopened for trade with the West in 1856, Japanese art and bric-a-brac—woodcut prints, kimonos, fans, lacquers, bronzes, and silks— flooded England, France, and America, prompting a period of Japonisme, or a craze for all things Japanese that influenced artists of the day.

naturalize—To grant full citizenship to.

nisei—Translates to "second-generation"; this term describes the son or daughter of an issei.

BIBLIOGRAPHY

Ashton, Dore. *Noguchi East and West*. Berkeley and Los Angeles, Calif.: University of California Press, 1992.

Bassett, Bruce W., dir. *The Creative Adventures of Isamu Noguchi*. VHS/DVD. Chicago, Ill.: Whitgate Productions, 1980.

Cort, Louise Allison, and Bert Winther-Tamaki. *Isamu Noguchi and Modern Japanese Ceramics, A Close Embrace of the Earth*. Washington, D.C.: The Arthur M. Sackler Gallery, Smithsonian Institution in association with University of California Press, 2004. [Monograph published in conjunction with 2004 exhibit.]

Cummings, Paul. *Artists in Their Own Words*. New York: St. Martin's Press, 1979.

Duus, Masayo. *The Life of Isamu Noguchi, Journey Without Borders*. Princeton and Oxford: Princeton University Press, 2004.

Gordon, John. *Isamu Noguchi*. New York: Praeger, 1968. [Monograph published in conjunction with Noguchi's first retrospective at the Whitney Museum of Art.]

Grove, Nancy. *Isamu Noguchi: Portrait Sculpture*. Washington, D.C.: Smithsonian Institution Press for the National Portrait Gallery, 1989.

Harth, Erica, ed. *Last Witnesses: Reflections on the Wartime Internment of Japanese Americans*. New York: Palgrave, 2001.

Hunter, Sam. *Isamu Noguchi*. Seattle, Wash.: University of Washington Press, 2000.

Noguchi, Isamu. *The Isamu Noguchi Garden Museum*. New York: Harry N. Abrams, 1987.

———. *A Sculptor's World*. New York: Harper & Row, 2004.

FURTHER READING

Hakutani, Yoshinobu, ed., *Selected English Writings of Yone Noguchi, An East-West Literary Assimilation, Volume I: Poetry.* Madison, N.J.: Fairleigh Dickinson University Press, 1990. (Poetry by Noguchi's father, a noted scholar)

———. *Selected English Writings of Yone Noguchi, An East-West Literary Assimilation, Volume II: Prose.* Fairleigh Dickinson University Press, 1992.

Narita, Hiro, dir. *Isamu Noguchi: Stones and Paper.* Part of the *American Masters* PBS series, 1997.

Tracy, Robert. *Spaces of the Mind: Isamu Noguchi's Dance Designs.* Pompton Plains, N.J.: Amadeus Press, Limelight Editions, 2001.

WEB SITES

Densho: The Japanese American Legacy Project. Available online. URL: http://www.densho.org/.

Japanese American Citizen's League. Available online. URL: http://www.jacl.org/.

Japanese American National Museum in Los Angeles. Available online. URL: www.janm.org.

The Japanese Garden Database. Available online. URL: http://www.jgarden.org.

The Knoll Museum. Available online. URL: http://www.knoll.com/museum/index.jsp.

The Museum of Modern Art. Available online. URL: http://www.moma.org.

"Nikkei Heritage." National Japanese American Historical Society. Available online. URL: http://www.njahs.org/.

The Noguchi Museum. Available online. URL: http://www.noguchi.org.

PICTURE CREDITS

INDEX

ABOUT THE AUTHOR

CAROLINE TIGER studied literature and art history at the University of Pennsylvania. She is currently a freelance journalist who contributes articles to many magazines. She is also the author of several books, with topics that range from etiquette to the American Revolution. She lives in Philadelphia and can be found online at http://www.carolinetiger.com.